GREEK
PHILOSOPHY

·K·U·P·E·R·A·R·D·

Published in Great Britain by
Kuperard, an imprint of Bravo Ltd
59 Hutton Grove, London N12 8DS
www.kuperard.co.uk
Enquiries: office@kuperard.co.uk

Series Editor Geoffrey Chesler
Design Bobby Birchall

ISBN 978 1 85733 488 3

British Library Cataloguing in Publication Data
A CIP catalogue entry for this book
is available from the British Library.

Printed in Malaysia

Cover image: *The School of Athens* (detail). Fresco by Raphael,
1510–11, in the Palace of the Vatican.

Images on the following pages reproduced under Creative
Commons Attribution licences 2.5/3: 27 © Vaggelis Vlahos;
93 © PHGCOM; 116 © Ricardo André Frantz; and
131 © Eric Gaba

GREEK PHILOSOPHY

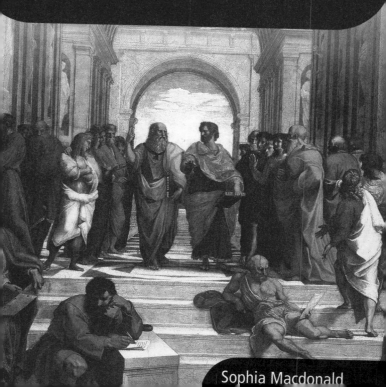

Sophia Macdonald

⊙ Contents

Map: The Greek World at the Time of Aristotle	6
1 Thinking and the Greeks	8
▪ What's the Point?	8
▪ What is Philosophy?	8
▪ What the Greeks meant by Philosophy	11
▪ Where did Greek Philosophy come from?	16
▪ How do we know about Ancient Greek Philosophy?	18
2 From Mythology to Philosophy	22
▪ Society and Philosophy	22
▪ The Homeric Epics and the Greek Dark Age	23
▪ The Development of the City-State	25
▪ Making Philosophy Possible	29
▪ What about Women Philosophers?	31
▪ Questioning Mythology	32
▪ The Seven Sages	36
▪ Herodotus and Thucydides	36
3 Thinking about the Universe	38
▪ Why 'Presocratic' Philosophers?	38
▪ Who were the Presocratics?	39
▪ Common Concerns	41
▪ The Milesian Pioneers	43
4 Pythagoras to Heraclitus	52
5 The Thinkers from Elea	66
6 Pluralists and Atomists	78
▪ Pluralist Theories	79
▪ The Atomists	87
7 Thinking for a Living – the Sophists	92
8 Socrates	102
▪ Who was Socrates?	103
▪ The Death of Socrates	105
▪ The Socratic Method	108
▪ Socrates' Philosophy	109
9 Plato	114
▪ Plato's Life	115
▪ Works	117
▪ The Dialogue Form	118
▪ Plato, Socrates and Others	119
▪ Plato's Thought	120

10 Aristotle   130
- Aristotle's Life   130
- Works   132
- Aristotle's Thought   132

11 Cynics, Stoics and Epicureans   148
- The Cynics   148
- The Stoics   149
- The Epicureans   152

12 What Happened Next   154
- Hellenistic Philosophy and Science   154
- The Philosophical Legacy of Greek Philosopy   157
- The Natural Sciences   158
- Ethics and Society   160
- Greek Philosophy in the Arts   160

Chronology   162
Glossary   164
Further Reading   165
Index   166
Acknowledgements   168

List of Illustrations

Rodin's *The Thinker*   13
View of the Parthenon on the Acropolis   21
The Golden Mask of Agamemnon, Mycenae, *c.* 1600 BCE   23
Bull's Head rhyton (drinking vessel), Knossos, Crete, *c.* 1600 BCE   24
Monument to the Spartans at Thermopylae   27
Heracles and Athena. Drinking vessel, 480–470 BCE   28
Dionysos sailing among dolphins. Drinking vessel, *c.* 530 BCE   35
Terracotta plate with birds and patterns, *c.* 600 BCE   50
Marble bust of Epicurus. Roman copy of Greek original   89
Early Athenian coin   93
Bust of Socrates. Roman copy of Greek original, Palermo   104
The Death of Socrates, by David   107
Bust of Plato in the Capitoline Museum, Rome   116
Head of Aristotle. Roman copy of Greek bronze   131
Marcus Aurelius as 'the philosopher-king', 161–180 CE   151
Alexander the Great at the battle of Issus. Mosaic from Naples   155

The Greek World at the Time of Aristotle

Rome

ITALY

Elea
Metapontum
Tarentum

MAGNA GRAECIA

Croton

Locri

SICILY

Acragas
Leontini

Syracuse

IONIAN
SEA

THRA

MACEDONIA

Stagira

EPIRUS

GREECE

AEGE
SEA

EUBOE

Thebes

Corinth
Elis
Megara

PELOPONNESUS

Sparta

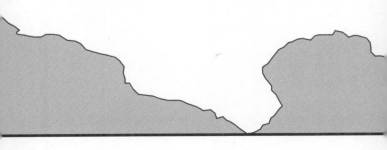

MEDITERRANEAN SEA

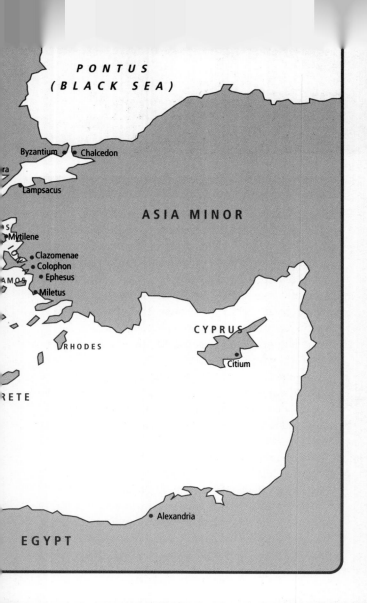

PONTUS
(BLACK SEA)

Byzantium • Chalcedon

Lampsacus

ra

ASIA MINOR

S

Mytilene

Clazomenae
Colophon
• Ephesus

AMOS

Miletus

RHODES

CYPRUS

Citium

RETE

• Alexandria

EGYPT

Chapter 1

Thinking and the Greeks

What's the Point?

Why should we be interested in ancient Greek philosophy? What is its relevance to us today? Indeed, why should we be interested in philosophy at all?

If we are interested in why our world is the way it is, in the nature of good and evil – even in the nature of the universe itself – we should be interested in philosophy in its broadest sense. Democracy, atoms, censorship, utopia – the Greeks thought about these things and many more, and their opinions have often proved prescient. Cynicism and Stoicism were Greek philosophical schools whose names have passed into common parlance to describe familiar human attitudes or attributes. What the Greeks called philosophy embraced what we would now call science as well as what we call ethics and political theory.

We should also be interested in philosophy if we are interested in history, for the two are closely intertwined. The great British philosopher Bertrand Russell taught that 'To understand an age or a nation, we must understand its philosophy.' Philosophies emerge from their particular societies, but, conversely, they feed back into those societies (even if in a very diluted form) and do much to determine their development. In particular, as we shall see later in this book, moral or ethical concepts cannot be understood without knowledge of the society that generated them.

What is Philosophy?

People have always been curious about the world they live in. The ancient Egyptians and Babylonians were making discoveries about mathematics and astronomy centuries before the first Greek thinkers we know of. Both the Chinese and the ancient peoples of Mesoamerica had developed systems of numbering and dating and made astronomical observations by the sixth to fifth centuries BCE. But it was with the Greeks that there began a shift from practical observation and recording to putting forward explanations for astronomical and physical phenomena deduced through reasoning.

The Greek word *philosophia*, from which the word 'philosophy' is derived, literally means 'love of wisdom'. That may sound easy and uncontroversial, but it is not: philosophers themselves have come up with many definitions, frequently contradictory, and as we shall see in this book, even the first philosophers of ancient Greece disagreed about what philosophy was and who was the best kind of person to be a philosopher. In the words of Plato in his dialogue *Phaedo*, 'For every philosopher there is an equal and opposite philosopher'. Yet, for a useful working definition, we might suggest that philosophy seeks to make sense of the world or the universe through reasoning and to arrive at a systematic and coherent world view.

In the 1940s, Russell called philosophy 'something intermediate between theology and science ... a No Man's Land, exposed to attack from both sides', a discipline which asks – even if it cannot answer – such questions as:

- Does the world consist of both mind and matter, and, if so, what part is mind and what part is matter?
- For that matter, what *is* mind?
- Has the universe any unity or purpose? Is it evolving towards any goal or with any purpose?
- Are there such things as laws of nature, and what are they?
- What is knowledge?
- What are good and evil? Are there universal definitions of them, or only subjective or relative ones?

Philosophy today deals with abstract concepts – goodness, evil, justice, freedom, love, knowledge, and the like – but we also encounter these concepts all the time in our everyday lives. Should I smack my child? Is theft ever justified? What are the pros and cons of the death penalty? Are sex and violence in entertainment a bad influence? How democratic is Western democracy? These are all questions that have no immediate, factual, 'right' answer, but which are relevant and can be explored by argument – that is, by the practical exercise of philosophy.

Perhaps it is the act of questioning and arguing that is the most common feature of definitions of philosophy. Philosophy does not take things at face value, and in particular, it does not accept dogma but rather subjects it to interrogation. In fact, philosophy can subvert established beliefs and behaviours by asking uncomfortable or forbidden questions. Whereas religion and law are based on authorities that are not meant to be questioned (for example, scriptures/holy writs, legal codes), a defining feature of philosophy is that it seeks to justify or refute statements by analysis of ideas, by reasoning, and by presenting arguments for its conclusions.

What the Greeks meant by Philosophy

Philosophy and science are nowadays separate disciplines, each with many subcategories, but in ancient Greece 'natural philosophers' studied mathematics, physics, logic, cosmology, biology and medicine, as well as politics, ethics, aesthetics, even literary criticism. A standard Greek definition of what a philosopher sought – what *philosophia* was – was 'knowledge of things human and things divine'; for the philosopher Heraclitus, around 500 BCE, 'philosophical

men must be versed in very many things'. By the time
of Aristotle, philosophy was regularly being classified
into a number of disciplines, including:

- **logic** (from *logos*, literally meaning a word or
  thought, but by extension 'reason', from *legein*, to
  say, tell, or explain): language, meaning, the study
  of thought and argument;
- **ethics** (from *ethos*, custom, and by extension moral
  character): the study of moral and political concepts,
  but also including what we would think of as
  sociology;
- **physics** (from *physis*, nature): the study of the
  phenomena of the natural world, including
  speculation about the physical origins and evolution
  of the universe;
- **metaphysics**: this refers to a set of ultimate
  questions about the nature of being, which
  preoccupied the Greek philosophers greatly from
  very early on but which did not acquire the name of
  'metaphysics' until centuries later. Aristotle called
  his own enquiries into this field 'First Philosophy'.

The earliest Greek philosophers were primarily
interested in what we would call natural sciences
rather than what we understand as 'philosophy': they
focused chiefly on **physics**, or an understanding of the
physical nature of the universe around them. They
were sometimes called 'natural philosophers'. They
turned an enquiring eye on everything from eclipses,
the heavenly bodies, and meteorological events to
living organisms and human beings themselves.

⊙ The Thinker. *Auguste Rodin, 1902. Musée Rodin, Paris.*

These were observable phenomena, and they used reasoning to speculate on them. They also thought about the nature and beginning of the universe, its constituent element or elements, and the causes of change and movement in the universe at large – preoccupations that are still with us today.

Perhaps the most valuable, and certainly the most durable, legacy the Greek philosophers have handed down to us is the method of **logic**, that is, of using reasoned argument to support a theory and arrive at a conclusion. This method began with the very first Greek thinker of whom we have any evidence, Thales (*c.* 625–*c.* 545 BCE; see chapter 3). Thales deduced, from his observations of the changes in the state of water to ice, steam and so on, that everything must be made of water. This was a very bold step: he was saying to his contemporaries, to whom the universe was incomprehensible, that he had discovered its secret and that, on the contrary, it was actually quite simple – just one material was the basis of it all. Later Presocratic philosophers (see chapter 3) such as Parmenides (born *c.* 515 BCE; see chapter 5) came to view intellectual argument – in explicit contradistinction to observation and perception by the senses, which he considered unreliable – as the only route to truth. The study of logic in Greece culminated (though it did not end) with the immensely influential work of Aristotle (384–322 BCE; see chapter 10).

As for **ethics**, we might expect moral thinking in the Greek world to be reflected in literature, which deals everywhere with human choices, motives and emotions. Much of Greek tragic drama, for instance, revolves around moral choices. But the reader or spectator soon becomes aware not only that ancient Greek ideas of morality were very different from our own, but also that their dramatic presentation does not in general constitute a reasoned discussion of the morality of a particular course of action – only the setting out of choices and the unfolding of consequences. Discussion of the nature of virtue and the good only gradually took on the characteristics of the study of ethics. The Pythagoreans and Heraclitus, for instance, expressed opinions on the mores of their society and made suggestions about beneficial practices, but they did not analyse them in detail – though they did have some interesting things to say about the concept of justice, often at the cosmological level. In the mid fifth century BCE the Sophists (see chapter 7) gave practical tuition to young aristocratic men in rhetoric and the skills necessary for public life, and, according to their disapproving contemporary Socrates, claimed to teach them virtue too. But it was only with Socrates that we can say that the systematic study of moral values and their reflection in human behaviour began in earnest.

The later Presocratic philosophers had an overriding interest in the field of enquiry that later became known as **metaphysics**. This sought to understand the 'why' of the universe, not just the 'what', 'when', 'where' and 'how'; it looked for some transcendental unifying principle or agent lying behind or beyond the material world we live in; and it speculated about the nature of existence itself (ontology). Although it is distinct from theology or religion, this field of speculation often saw this principle as divine. Parmenides' theory of the One and Plato's theory of Forms (see chapter 9) are key examples of this kind of thinking.

The philosophical conclusions of the Greek thinkers were not always right – in fact, viewed from today's perspective, they were nearly always wrong and sometimes positively bizarre; but the great achievement, and one that underlies all subsequent Western philosophy, is that they were arrived at in a process that we recognize today as scientific. They relied on argument, deduction and proof to support their hypotheses, not simply assertion backed by some kind of (not necessarily intellectual) authority. Moreover, their explanations were efficient and economical: they strove to explain the universe in terms of its own internal features, and with recourse to as few hypothetical substances (water, air) and processes (rarefaction, condensation, 'strife') as possible.

Essentially, they did what modern science also tries to do – 'to explain as much as possible in terms of as little as possible' – and they were the first to do it.

Where did Greek Philosophy come from?

I have suggested that the Greeks invented philosophy. But, of course, philosophy didn't appear fully-fledged out of nowhere in the sixth century BCE; neither was intellectual life in Greece non-existent before Thales. Poets and dramatists both before and contemporary with the Presocratics had thought about nature and the origins of the universe; in the eighth century Hesiod (c. 740–670 BCE) had written a long poem, the *Theogony*, which gave a mythographic account of the creation of the earth, the solar system and the gods in a series of generations going back to original Chaos. Although the Presocratic philosophers reacted against explanations such as this and sought rational

explanations instead, the influence of mythical
elements is traceable in many of them.

The Greek dramatists spoke often of the soul, but
they did not investigate its existence or nature, which
were key objects of analysis to their philosophical
contemporaries. But they were aware of philosophical
ideas and – naturally – often acquainted with the
philosophers themselves. There is a story in which
Euripides gave Socrates a copy of Heraclitus' book
and asked his opinion of it (Socrates replied that what
he understood of it was splendid, and he would have
to imagine that the parts he didn't understand must
be splendid too). The comic playwright Aristophanes
knew enough about Socrates and his ideas to be able
to lampoon him astutely in *The Clouds*. Plato is said to
have been a playwright before he took up philosophy,
which may partly explain why he couched his ideas in
the dramatic dialogue form. The works of the
historians Herodotus and Thucydides (see chapter 2)
contained analysis as well as narration: Herodotus
was interested in natural phenomena and in the
meeting of different cultures, and both were
interested in human motivation and causation, for
instance as regards war. The well-travelled Herodotus
must also have been influential in introducing new
ideas about the variety of experience and customs in
other lands, giving further food for thought to
contemporary philosophers.

Beyond Greece, to the south and east, were other
sources of scientific thought. The Greek alphabet
itself, which made the writing of literature possible, is
an adaptation of the alphabet of Phoenicia in what we

now call the Middle East. It was no accident that the first scientific speculations emerged not from the Greek mainland but from Ionia, on the west coast of what is now Turkey. Relations of trade and diplomacy between Ionia and the eastern countries, especially Babylonia, would have fostered cultural and intellectual exchanges. Babylonian astronomy, already advanced by Thales' time, must have been known to the Ionians and stimulated their own investigations – Thales' knowledge of an eclipse (see chapter 3) is a case in point. Egypt was also influential, principally as the wellspring of mathematics: so much so that later Greek writers routinely assumed that the early philosophers had visited Egypt or studied there, whether or not they had actually done so. But there are also elements in the earliest Greek thought that cannot be traced to the Egyptians or the Babylonians and must therefore be assumed to be original to Greece. Chief among those is the approach that attempted to explain the world systematically through rational argument based on observation without recourse to mythological explanations.

How do we know about Ancient Greek Philosophy?

This book deals in greater detail with Socrates, Plato and Aristotle than with any of their predecessors or contemporaries. There are two interrelated reasons for this. First, they were the most influential of all philosophers, not only in their own time, but for many centuries afterwards; second, in the case of Plato and

Aristotle, more of their writings have survived than of any other ancient Greek philosophers. Both men set up schools of learning that lasted in one form or another for several centuries; their works then passed into early and medieval Christian theology and philosophy, where they were translated, discussed, absorbed and adapted. Plato's dialogues, our main source for the ideas of Socrates as well as Plato's own thought, have survived almost in their entirety. The large number of works we have by Aristotle have survived for similar reasons, though it is estimated that they represent only about a third of his actual output. Aristotle was also translated and studied by Arabic scholars, so he has come down to us by more than one route.

Apart from these three great figures, however, the record is frustratingly thin. The works of the Presocratic philosophers survive only fragmentarily, in quotations by other writers. The nearest thing to a complete history of philosophy that survives from the ancient world was written by Diogenes Laertius, a scholar in the early third century CE. More a compendium of quotations from the philosophers than an analytic work, it is none the less the most important biographical source, particularly for the Presocratics, that we have. The sixth-century philosopher Simplicius, who studied at Alexandria and Athens and wrote vast commentaries on Aristotle's works, is another important supplier of information of the Presocratics, but even by his time their texts were disappearing. Aristotle himself, having an interest in the history of philosophy and science, is a major source of knowledge of many of his predecessors, for instance in the *Physics*, *Metaphysics* and *On Democritus*.

It is hard not to feel that we are peering at the ancient Greek philosophers though several veils. They have been quoted, discussed and criticized by many different writers in many different genres, over many centuries. The gulf of time and the radical differences between ancient Greek culture and our own are no small obstacles to our understanding. Also, the utterances of early thinkers tend to be quoted by later ones in the form of sayings or maxims rather than extended, coherent discussions. Even assuming that these fragmentary texts have been accurately filtered through the secondary sources and not misinterpreted, misquoted or distorted by later writers struggling to clarify – or to co-opt – the arguments of the early Greek thinkers, this lack of context in itself makes them elusive. And, as often as not, they were just obscure – Heraclitus, for instance, was famously enigmatic even in his own day – because they were wrestling with new concepts and a new method, and in the process creating a new vocabulary in which to express them. Yet, through all the veils, it is impossible to encounter these thinkers without catching the scent of the excitement and the joy in discovery that they must have felt on their diverse journeys towards making sense of their world.

This book is not a philosophy textbook. It won't teach you how to think like Plato or Aristotle. But it will introduce you to them and their predecessors and contemporaries, it will try to show you how Greek

philosophy developed and what we owe to it, and
I hope it will excite your curiosity and stimulate you
to further exploration.

⌄ *The Parthenon on the Acropolis, dedicated to the goddess Athena.*
Fifth century BCE

Chapter 2

From Mythology to Philosophy

Society and Philosophy

We remarked in chapter 1 that philosophical ideas cannot be separated from the societies that produced them. Greek philosophy originated in a particular moment in Greek history, the sixth century, when the society that had produced the Homeric *Iliad* and *Odyssey* and the didactic poems of Hesiod two centuries earlier was mutating into a society where rational, scientific enquiry into the natural world could happen.

Very broadly, this development was due to three factors:

- the recovery and socialization of writing after the Dark Age and an increasingly literate society;
- trade, leading to increasing prosperity and the growth of a leisured class in many places, and bringing contact with new ideas, in particular scientific ideas;
- a growing diversity in the forms of government and social organization of the Greek city-states from the sixth century on, fostering a corresponding diversity of concepts of social function and a shift in perceptions of the function of individuals in society.

The Homeric Epics and the Greek Dark Age

The Homeric epic poems depict a society consisting of many small kingdoms, constantly feuding. The human heroes who people the *Iliad* come together to fight in the Trojan war not because of any notion of a united Greece but for the honour, glory and revenge that will strengthen, or recover, their social function as kings and warriors. Social relations are rigidly hierarchical, with a warrior king at the top in each kingdom, ruling an aristocratic elite whose chief activity is fighting and whose status, virtue, and honour are defined by their success in battle. Below this elite class come peasant farmers and slaves. In this society, to be 'good' means to fulfil your social function well: the behaviour of Achilles, Agamemnon, Menelaus and the other kings in the *Iliad* may be, to modern eyes, cruel, petulant, even childish, yet they are regularly described as *agathos*, 'good', because in Homer a 'good' king or warrior is good if he fulfils the social function of being a king or a warrior well.

Though seen through 'a haze of legend', as Bertrand Russell puts it, this picture does tell us something about the reality of the period when the epics were growing. This period, known today as the Dark Age of Greece, is generally dated from about 1150 to about 800 BCE; the Homeric epics were arguably its greatest cultural artefact. Evidence explaining the sudden onset of the Dark Age is scanty, but it seems to have been precipitated by a combination of aggressive migration by Greek-speaking Dorians from the north and, possibly, environmental disaster. In any event, the sophisticated, palace-centred culture built by the Mycenaeans up to about 1200 collapsed, many towns were abandoned, writing was forgotten, and the lively trade network shrivelled – though many Greeks emigrated to the western coast of Asia Minor and set up communities, such as Miletus, there. According to the archaeological evidence, the depopulated Greek archipelago sank back into subsistence agriculture, carried on in scattered communities each centred on a village and headed by, in effect, a warlord, aided by either a council of elders or (as in Sparta) a military elite.

When the Homeric epics were finally written down, towards the very end of the Dark Age, the society they describe was already becoming antiquated. The poems had taken shape over several centuries by a process of repetition, accretion and modification, being recited and handed on by generations of bards. Their style of composition was highly formulaic, rather like that of a narrative folk ballad. Around the early to mid eighth century BCE, the Phoenician alphabet was brought to

Greece and adapted to the Greek language, and it is likely that this was the moment at which the Homeric poems were set in writing and took the final form in which they have come down to us today.

Hesiod's *Works and Days*, a poem probably roughly contemporary with the writing down of the Homeric epics, gives us glimpses into the life of an eighth-century Greek farmer. Hesiod is the first Greek author to tell us anything about himself, and what he tells us is illuminating, for he appears not to have been an aristocrat: he was a shepherd, and his father had been a merchant seaman. The archaeological evidence suggests that by this time the country was recovering in population and prosperity and Greeks were ranging far afield as traders. This was the period in which several Greek cities founded colonies in Sicily and southern Italy, and existing contacts with the east expanded.

At this time there was still no such thing as 'Greece': no unified nation, just a collection of separate communities, isolated from each other by mountains and the broken coastline. Reurbanization had gradually taken off towards the end of the Dark Age, and between the eighth century and the sixth, these communities developed into more consolidated and organized, but still autonomous, city-states, each consisting of one or more urban centres with its surrounding farmland and hamlets.

The Development of the City-State

The development of the city-state or *polis* (from which we get 'politics') was a significant change, but one that we can see emerging from Dark Age forms of socio-political organization. Monarchies gradually gave way in most places to oligarchies of one kind or another, and the growing population of small landowners described by Hesiod began to demand, and win, greater participation in the government of their cities. This expanded group became known as the *politai*, members of the *polis*. The word *polites* has traditionally been translated as 'citizen', but citizenship was very limited by present-day standards, since it excluded women, landless men and slaves. During the sixth and fifth centuries BCE, despite attempts at regulation, slavery became widespread, propelled by the development of industry and the expansion of wealth; people could be born into slavery or become slaves through being captured in war or piracy. Slave markets flourished in several of the countries on the fringes of Greece and in Asia Minor.

As independent, self-governing units, the city-states began to develop in different ways, but Sparta diverged most drastically from the rest of Greece, and especially from Athens, which became its chief rival, the rivalry eventually breaking into open warfare in the long Peloponnesian War of 431–404 BCE. Whereas Athens was relatively undisturbed by the Dorian invasion, keeping much of its original population and way of life, Sparta was completely settled by Dorians, who reduced the indigenous population to serfdom as helots. Sparta remained agricultural and had no significant commercial class. It was highly militarized, but developed communal values and practices such as the collective education of children. (Much later, in the first century CE, the philosopher and biographer Plutarch likened Spartan society to that of bees.) Women in Sparta were not secluded, and girls did gymnastic training together with boys; but their primary function was always as child-bearers, and they took no part in government. But then, neither did helots or the rural population of Laconia, the land around the city of Sparta.

Sparta's political institutions were complex and full of mechanisms for mutual accountability (there were, for instance, two kings, only one of whom went to war at any one time); by about the seventh century, they were very different from those of the other Greek states. Five magistrates called ephors (*ephoroi*) were chosen more or less by lot from the whole citizenry; their functions included monitoring the behaviour of the kings, especially in war. Tradition said that Sparta's constitution had been introduced by the lawgiver  Lycurgus in the ninth century, but he may have been a mythical figure; archaeological evidence puts the introduction of Sparta's institutions closer to 600.

As Sparta became increasingly militarized from the seventh century onward, its intellectual culture waned, and it is not surprising that no important philosopher came from Sparta in the Classical period. The only one we know of was Chilon, one of the Seven Sages (see below), but he seems to owe that honour more to his political services than to any contribution to philosophy. More crucial for the history of philosophy is the influence the city's customs and political system had on thinking about politics. In fact the image was more influential than the reality. An idealized aura of simple and beautiful austerity grew up around Sparta – encouraged, no doubt, by envy of its spectacular military success, but not really reflective of the difficult and often brutal reality. Plato was a particular admirer, as we shall see in chapter 9.

Athens, on the other hand, like most city-states, suffered far more internal conflict than the stable but relentlessly conservative Sparta, whose system hardly changed for centuries. Athens was beset with frequent, violent changes of government, seesawing from democracy to tyranny and back again several times between the establishment of an early form of democracy by Solon in 594 and its final subjugation by the Macedonians in 323. None the less, Athens' material prosperity and political ambitions increased, as did its population, and it became Greece's most important cultural centre, the vast intellectual energy of the Classical period seemingly nourished by political strife and change. But Athens, too, depended on social inequities, in particular the seclusion of women and the subjugation of slaves. Around 430 BCE slaves made up probably over a third of the population of the region of Attica.

Making Philosophy Possible

Through the resurgence of trade, the colonization of lands to the east and west, and the Persian wars of the first half of the fifth century, contact with other societies showed the Greeks that there were different ways of doing things and of understanding moral values. The distinction, as regards moral and political values and practices, between what people thought true in one place but not another and what appeared to be universally true, became more and more evident. This realization underlies the concept of relativism, which was more systematically explored by the Sophists (see chapter 7).

The increasing material wealth that came from industry and trade also made it possible for some people at least to have time for thinking and discussion. The creation of the leisured class for whom philosophy was considered a suitable occupation depended on the growth of economic relations according to which some people lived at leisure while others – women, slaves, peasants – worked.

In fact the existence of a leisured class who did not need to work generated a characteristic of Greek thinking that is perhaps unique, at least in the ancient world. That is the great value the Greeks placed on uselessness. This may seem a strange assertion, but we find it, for instance, in the view that the highest form of activity at the Olympic Games – higher even than competing – was the intellectual activity of watching. In architecture, they valued perfection of form much more than practicality; you could say they invented the idea of beauty. They saw themselves as intellectually superior to other peoples. But it was not until Thales that they began to intellectualize the kind of reasoning that had been applied to solving practical problems and apply it to questions of no practical value, such as the nature of the universe. They asked questions for the sake of asking questions, and they engaged in thinking for sheer pleasure.

This could not have happened in a purely rural society. Creative leisure and intellectual life were really possible only within a city, where the population was concentrated and people could meet and exchange ideas – in short, where they could *debate*. The method of philosophical argument that is the particular invention of the Greeks could only be practised in an urban setting. The city was inseparable from the act of philosophizing. Political developments were determinant, too, in this respect: the emergence of more democratic forms of government in the city-states meant that debate became a necessary tool of governance. Greek society became one in which the formation and expression of ideas mattered.

So, when Greek philosophers began to discuss the role of human beings in the world, they automatically took the city as the fundamental social unit rather than, for instance, the family. The virtuous life was seen in terms of the dutiful exercise of citizenship and the individual's relation to the city-state, rather than one's responsibility to other people in the family or any other social unit. Plato, in fact, thought the family a breeding-ground for selfishness and an obstacle to the citizen's full identification with his [*sic*] community. His ideal society was an ideal *city*; he could not imagine any other kind of society. In such a world view, and particularly with Plato and Aristotle, who provide us with the most detailed theoretical investigation of Greek political life that we have, ethics and politics were closely intertwined.

❯❯ What about Women Philosophers?

In the Greek city-state, only citizens mattered, and only free men could be citizens and hence thinkers. The way mythological women such as Helen of Troy, Medea, Electra or Antigone are portrayed in drama, as powerful seductresses or avatars of vengeance, sharply misrepresents the hard facts of women's generally secluded lives in Classical Greece. Only a few philosophers turned their gaze on women at all. Pythagoras (see chapter 4) admitted women and men on equal terms into his communal society, and Plato allowed women into his ideal society as warriors and philosophers, though not apparently out of any sense of equality. Both Pythagoras' and Plato's proposals about women were regarded at the time as either dangerously radical or hilarious. Aristotle's view of women is more typical, but makes chilling reading to a modern audience: he regarded women as *naturally* inferior, saying in his *Politics* that 'the relationship between the male and the female is by nature such that the male is higher, the female lower, that the male rules and the female is ruled'.

However, there do seem to have been some Greek women thinkers. The chief source of evidence for this is a seventeenth-century Frenchman, Gilles Ménage, who trawled the extant texts of Herodotus, Plato, Aristotle, Diogenes Laertius, Plutarch and many later authors in search of proof that, contrary to long-held opinion, there had been women philosophers in ancient Greece. His *History of Women Philosophers*, published in 1690, named some twenty women thinkers in the period between the twelfth century BCE and the death of Aristotle. Several of them were Pythagoreans.

Both Plato and Aristotle take the city as political and ethical model so much for granted that their works show no awareness of the fact that, by their time, the city-state was already in decline. The seams of the Athenian *polis* had begun to creak when Athens lost the Peloponnesian war to Sparta in 404, and the ensuing political upheavals led, among other things, to the execution of Socrates in 399. The whole Greek region was defeated by Philip of Macedon in Aristotle's lifetime; Aristotle had himself tutored Philip's son, the future Alexander the Great. With the Macedonian conquest the city was dislodged from its position as the centre of social, political and moral life. As political boundaries became more distant, a more individualistic, less socially oriented world view grew up, for instance among the Stoics and Cynics (see chapter 11), who argued in different ways for the emotional and political self-sufficiency of the wise individual.

Questioning Mythology

Social and political change and wider contacts with other cultures around the Mediterranean led, by the early sixth century, to a questioning of the myths that formed the basis of Greek religion and belief. In particular, an urge to understand the origins of the universe and the causes of natural phenomena grew up. Explanations based on the activities of the gods no longer seemed to fill the bill. This was a key preoccupation of the Presocratic philosophers. Not that they were atheists – far from it: some of them were very pious, one at least, Empedocles, boasting that he himself was a god. But they questioned the belief that the gods had *created* life or *caused* natural phenomena. They proposed, for the first time in their civilization, that thunder was not caused by Zeus or earthquakes by Poseidon. They wanted to explain the physical universe by physical means.

A clash of cosmogonies (accounts of the origins of the universe) must also have contributed to this questioning. Traditional Greek myths of origin, such as we find in Homer and in Hesiod's *Theogony* (Birth of the Gods), said (with some variations) that the first thing to exist was Chaos, the Void, from which were born Nyx (Night), Erebus (Darkness), and Gaea (Earth). Gaea and Uranus (Heaven) bore a multitude of offspring, the Titans, including Kronos (Time), who castrated and banished Uranus and later became the father of Zeus. In his turn Zeus led his own siblings in a war against their father and the other Titans; once victorious, the younger generation of gods settled on Mount Olympus with Zeus as their supreme ruler. Many abstract concepts and emotions – Anger, Strife, Sleep, Peace, and so on – were personified as gods and goddesses.

Then, some time between the seventh and fifth centuries, a new religion entered the Greek lands from Thrace to the north, claiming Orpheus (who may or may not have been a real person) as its founder. Though it incorporated many Greek figures, its story of creation was different, with Kronos at the head, generating Phanes, creator and first king of the gods, from an egg formed in the aether, and with Dionysus or

Zagreus (also known as Bacchus), a son of Zeus, as the key focus of worship. Most importantly, unlike the Homeric version, Orphism also gave an account of the creation of human beings: it told how the Titans had killed and eaten the child Dionysus, but one of Zeus's siblings had rescued the child's heart, which Zeus swallowed and then regenerated by coupling with Semele. Zeus punished the Titans for their crime by blasting them with lightning; from their ashes human beings were formed. Plato refers to a proverbial saying about humanity's 'Titanic nature', meaning the innate evil in human nature: humans contain both earthly and divine elements because they are made out of the ashes of the Titans who had devoured the divine child Dionysus.

Orphism suggested something about human nature, and the mixture of good and evil in it, that the religion of the Olympians did not. In its early form, the worship of Dionysus allowed people to express their emotions in violent, possibly trance-induced mystical dance. Women played a large role. The effect all this must have had on more orthodox city fathers was dramatized in Euripides' tragedy *The Bacchae*. Later, followers of Orphism lived in religious communities, not family groups, to which both men and women were admitted on equal terms. From their influence arose the concept of philosophy as a *way of life*, which we shall see put into practice by the Pythagoreans.

The new cult of Dionysus did not displace the traditional religion, but it must have shaken unquestioning adherence to it. When these two different cosmogonies came face to face, doubt was cast on the long-accepted stories of the first beginnings. Here were new stories to explain the same thing. What if they were all just stories? The Presocratic philosophers ran with this idea. By seeking a physical explanation of the beginning of the universe they were implicitly rejecting the idea that any divine being had created it. They did not deny that there was order in the world – indeed it was the source of that order that they sought – but they did question whether the order was divine, and looked for the explanation in terms of the world itself, not some external, anthropomorphic agent. This meant discovering non-theological *causation*, the search for which is one of the pervasive themes of Presocratic philosophy.

Under these several influences, Presocratic philosophy developed in two major strands: thinking about the physical nature and origin of the universe and its contents, on the one hand, and thinking about humanity, politics, justice, good and evil, the existence and nature of the soul, the human relationship with the divine, and the best way to live, on the other. The first generation of Presocratics, whom we shall meet in the next chapter, were principally materialists, but before long human concerns began to claim the attention of thinkers as well. We end this chapter with some other figures who were not strictly speaking philosophers but who made important contributions to philosophy.

The Seven Sages

The men traditionally referred to as the Seven Sages of Greece were philosophers, statesmen and legislators of the late seventh and the sixth centuries BCE. Exactly who was on the list was never quite agreed in antiquity; but Plato refers, in the context of Spartan education and its admirers, to Thales, Pittacus of Mytilene, Bias of Priene, Solon of Athens (often called the father of Athenian democracy), Cleobulus of Lindus, Myson of Chenae, and Chilon of Sparta. Except for Thales, they were not really philosophers in the modern sense, but practical politicians. However, in that respect their speeches and sayings can be seen as ultimate precursors of the Classical period's greatest thinkers about ethics, politics and morality: Socrates, Plato and Aristotle.

Herodotus and Thucydides

Herodotus (c. 484–c. 425 BCE) and Thucydides (c. 455–c. 400 BCE) were the principal historians of Classical Greece.

Herodotus was a native of Halicarnassus in Ionia (modern Bodrum) but spent much of his adult life travelling in Greece and abroad – by his own account he visited Egypt, Gaza, Babylonia, Scythia and the Bosporus region – before settling in the Athenian colony of Thurii. He wrote during the mid fifth century BCE, but his subject was the history of the Archaic period (c. 750–480 BCE), and his underlying theme was the meeting of the Greek world with the cultures of

Asia Minor, the Near East and Egypt. His work shares some of the preoccupations of the Presocratic philosophers in its fascination with the nature of different human cultures and the underlying causes of human actions, especially warfare, without reference to gods or divine will. His style tends to be anecdotal rather than analytical, and he is often very naïve, but his curiosity and questioning attitude, and his attention to all sides of an issue, using both Greek and non-Greek sources, link him methodologically with the Presocratics. He has become known as the father of history.

Thucydides, by contrast, concentrated on a wholly Greek subject, the Peloponnesian War between Athens and Sparta of 431–404 BCE. He was an Athenian, but had property in the mining district of Thrace, and was a military officer as well as a writer. When he failed to save the town of Amphipolis from Spartan attack he was exiled and stayed away for twenty years, during which he observed the war from both sides. He had begun, he says, to write his five-volume history of the war shortly after it started, but did not finish it; that task fell to three other writers. Thucydides was a much more analytical historian than Herodotus. He was not always right, and he was sympathetic not only towards the Athenian side on which he fought, but to Athens' general in the struggle, Pericles. But he did investigate conscientiously and report faithfully; his story does not shy away from Athens' defeat; and he brilliantly unravels the complex processes of decision-making or failure to decide that determined the fortunes of the parties in the war. For a long time he was called the pioneer of 'scientific history'.

Chapter 3

Thinking about the Universe

Why 'Presocratic' Philosophers?

The first period of what we can really call philosophy in Greece is traditionally known as the Presocratic period. It stretched from 585 (the date of Thales' observation of the eclipse, and one of the few exact dates we can give with confidence about the development of Greek philosophy) to about 400 BCE. The name 'Presocratic' is a little misleading, however: Socrates died in 399 BCE, so the period that is supposed to precede him spans all but the very last year of his life, and many of the 'Presocratics' were in fact his contemporaries, even his juniors.

Socrates is seen as the watershed for a variety of reasons, none of them totally convincing. One view is that he marked the shift of focus in Greek thought from the origin and nature of the universe to questions concerning human nature. But this is not entirely true: several Presocratic philosophers examined human questions (though in a different way from Socrates), and neither did Greek thinking about the physical universe cease just before Socrates – in fact it culminated well after Socrates' lifetime in Aristotle. What does seem to be new with Socrates is method, the dialectical process of question and answer that we

see in Plato. Even here there is a precedent in Socrates'
contemporaries, the Sophists; yet we can discern a
qualitative difference between Plato (who includes
Socrates, since Socrates reaches us through Plato) and
Aristotle and those who came before them. The
difference is also quantitative, since we have so much
more of the actual texts of Plato and Aristotle than we
do of any Presocratic philosopher. Everything we know
of the Presocratics is seen through the eyes of others –
but then, the same is true of Socrates. In the end, we
have to accept that the watershed is an artificial one
devised by scholars as an aid to tidy classification, so
we shall use it here.

Who were the Presocratics?

Historians of Greek philosophy from the earliest times
have liked to organize its development according to
'successions' of teachers and pupils and *their* pupils, or
in schools. So the Presocratic philosophers tend to be
grouped in successions centred on a place or a leading
figure, even if the members of the group don't always
agree. We know less about philosophical institutions
among the Presocratics than we do for later, better
documented periods. It is probably more appropriate

to use the term 'group' here rather than 'school', to distinguish them from the later schools founded by Plato and Aristotle, which have been called the first universities in Europe, and which were probably more systematic as institutions than anything earlier except the communities of the Pythagoreans (see chapter 4). However, it is convenient to discuss the Presocratics in groups, as Milesians or Ionians, Pythagoreans, Eleatics, Pluralists, Atomists and Sophists.

None of the earliest philosophers came from Athens. They all hailed from one or another of the small city-states on the shores of the Aegean that had at the time no political ties with Athens but were definitely part of the Greek world. The first three pioneers – Thales, Anaximander and Anaximenes – were all natives of Miletus in Ionia. Other Ionians came from Colophon, Ephesus, the island of Samos, and Clazomenae. A second important cradle of thought was Sicily and southern Italy (Croton, Elea, Acragas). Philosophy entered European Greece only with Democritus of Abdera, and the first philosopher who actually lived in Athens, although he was not born there, was Anaxagoras.

What kind of communication occurred between these dispersed thinkers? There is little direct evidence of contact between them, but many of them travelled or migrated in the course of their lives. Parmenides and Zeno were said to have visited Athens, and Anaxagoras spent much of his life there before exile in Lampsacus (in north-western Turkey, near modern Lapseki). These three were contemporaries – might they have met in Athens? We can only guess at it.

We can conclude that Thales, Anaximander and Anaximenes, who all lived in the same city at much the same time, would have known each other: sources say that Anaximander was a kinsman and pupil of Thales, and Anaximenes was probably a pupil or associate of Anaximander. But, apart from the Pythagorean communities, which are a rather special case, it is only with Plato that we get a vivid image of a group of men sitting or walking together, deep in debate. We don't even really know if thinkers from different cities wrote to each other or read each other's works, although here and there comparison of the texts show that one writer is quoting another.

Common Concerns

Whether or not there were direct contacts between the Presocratics, there is no doubt that they shared many interests. In particular they sought some single, underlying, primordial substance from which everything else in existence was derived – an alternative to mythological accounts of the beginning of the world. As Aristotle noted in his *Metaphysics*, 'most of the first philosophers thought that material principles alone were principles of all things.' They had varying ideas of what the primordial substance was; but they could scarcely even have conceptualized a single origin for the universe if they had not already formed a concept of the universe as an ordered whole whose order could be determined: it was neither the creation of some god or divine force nor a disordered mess intractable to intelligent explanation. The word they used for this order was *kosmos*, a word cognate with *kosmeuein*, to arrange or set in order. Heraclitus is probably the first Greek thinker to use *kosmos* clearly in this specific sense of the ordered world. The early Presocratics also argued that the world was governed by some regulatory force; this idea lies behind Anaximander's notion of cosmic justice, which maintains balance in the universe. Heraclitus and Parmenides were also concerned with cosmic justice.

Mathematics was an important part of Presocratic philosophy. The Greeks traditionally regarded Egypt as the wellspring of mathematics, but it was they who applied deductive reasoning to it. According to Russell, mathematics was influential not only as the basis of a form of argument but as 'the chief source of the belief in self-evident and exact truth': by dealing with the ideal forms of physical objects (nothing in nature, for instance, is as perfectly circular as the exact geometrical diagram of a circle) it opened the way for the idea that thought could tell one more than sense-perception and hence that the objects of theory were more real than sensible objects. Thales introduced the notion of mathematical proof and made some basic geometrical discoveries. Mathematics was central to the Pythagorean movement: numerous discoveries in geometry and music, including the famous theorem about the square on the hypotenuse, have been attributed to Pythagoreans (rather than to Pythagoras himself). Among other things, the Pythagoreans proved the existence of 'irrational' numbers, with a drastic effect on the rest of their theory of the universe (see chapter 4).

We hear little if anything about human life and moral values from the early Presocratics, except in their capacity as politicians. Most of them, being aristocratic or propertied citizens, were active in the government of their cities or as military leaders; but mere practical political advice hardly counts as philosophizing. But, as time went on, theoretical speculation on political concepts, such as the nature of justice, grew increasingly important to ancient philosophers, becoming central to Plato's thought. An interest in human life and motivation does surface quite early, with Pythagoras and his followers. The Pythagoreans were primarily interested in the soul, and believed in reincarnation. Their view of philosophy as a way of life, too, shows where their main interests lay. On the whole, however, even the later Presocratics were not explicitly interested in ethical theory, though they did concern themselves with theories of mind, its distinction from matter, and the nature of knowledge.

The Milesian Pioneers

Late-seventh-century Miletus must have been an exciting and dangerous place to be. One of the great Ionian cities, it was a neighbour to the powerful empires of Lydia and, after 546 when the Persians conquered the Lydian lands, Persia. It was particularly strong as a military and merchant naval power, which gave rise to its long rivalry with Lydia. It traded in many commodities – iron, timber, fish and wool are all mentioned; and its commercial network, plus its many colonies along the Bosporus, Black Sea, and Thrace, and its connections with Sybaris in Southern Italy, made it a cosmopolitan city where ideas and influences from many cultures must have met. Its politics were turbulent: Thales and his successors, Anaximander and Anaximenes, were born into a wealthy city periodically upset by internal conflict. They were chiefly concerned with cosmology, mathematics and astronomy.

THALES

(c. 625–c. 545 BCE)

One of the Seven Sages of Greece (see chapter 2), Thales was a practical politician and a military strategist as well as a natural philosopher. We have a few details of his life: Herodotus tells how during a military campaign he devised a way for King Croesus' army to ford a river by diverting its channel; the less reliable but entertaining biographer Diogenes Laertius makes him the subject of the world's first absent-minded professor joke: Thales tripped and fell into a ditch while stargazing, whereupon the woman who was with him exclaimed, 'Thales, how can you expect to see what's going on in the sky if you can't see what's in front of your own feet?'

Thales probably wrote no books, although various later commentators credit him with some writings. Aristotle and others attribute to him a number of mathematical discoveries, such as that a circle is bisected by its diameter and the angles at the base of an isosceles triangle are equal, and with some astronomical findings. But he is most famous for having observed – or perhaps predicted (the sources vary) – the first accurately datable event in Greek history: a solar eclipse on 28 May 585 BCE. His interest in eclipses could well have sprung from Miletus' links with Lydia, and through Lydia with Babylonia, where eclipses had long been studied by astronomers, so this story is quite credible.

Where Thales is widely considered to have broken new ground is in his theory that water was the original substance out of which everything else was created. Irrespective of its accuracy, this bold hypothesis is interesting because, for the first time, we have a reasoned argument to support a theory, based on Thales' empirical observation not only of the behaviour of water itself (freezing, evaporation, thawing), which caused it to change from one thing to another and reverse the process while still being demonstrably water, but of the reliance of all life on water for nourishment. Neither was this such a foolish hypothesis: we now know that a great many natural objects, including ourselves, consist largely of water. And in it lies the germ of the long strand of thinking that there has to be a single source of the component matter of the universe. Thales' realization that a substance could change without losing its essential nature was also important; and it was an idea carried forward by Anaximenes, the youngest of our three pioneers, in his concept of rarefaction and condensation in the universe.

Thales also held that the earth floats on water, like a floating log. He may have got this idea from seeing floating reed islands, which, according to Pliny, existed in Lydia. However, he did not explain what the water itself rests on, or whether it is limitless, as might have been appropriate for the primordial substance. Aristotle spotted the problem, remarking in his account of this theory that 'water cannot rest in mid-air – it must rest on something'. Although Thales seems never to have made any reference to the mythical origins of the universe, this image may hark back to the mythological Ocean that was believed to surround the earth. Some think Thales exemplifies the transition from mythology to science and philosophy, a view supported by Aristotle's remark that Thales thought everything was 'full of gods'. Thales probably did think that all things had souls, but he argued for this claim using the example of a magnet and its capacity to attract (i.e. to 'move') iron. Again, it is the process of reasoning that is important from a present-day standpoint, not the fact that the conclusion was wrong.

ANAXIMANDER

(*c.* 610–*c.* 540 bce)

We know nothing of Anaximander's life apart from his probable dates of birth and death and that he was also a Milesian, some twenty years younger than Thales and possibly his student. Among various 'firsts' with which he is credited, he is said to have written the first Greek treatise in prose rather than the poetic form in which all literature had been composed until then.

Venturing further down the path Thales had opened, Anaximander proposed that the universe not only originated in a single primordial substance but was subject to a single law. Unlike Thales, however, he posited that this substance, the material principle of everything that exists, was not any familiar earthly substance but something that he called *to apeiron*, 'the boundless'. Anaximander believed that everything in the world derived from four elements – air, earth, water and fire – that existed necessarily as pairs of opposites. But he disagreed with Thales' view that any of the four could be the underlying substance on its own, because each of them needed its opposite to maintain its existence. Beyond the four elements, he argued, there had to be something that had no opposite; accordingly he hypothesized the *apeiron*.

As well as being limitless in extent, the *apeiron* was 'eternal and ageless', 'ungenerated and indestructible', and from it came the heavens and 'all the worlds'. Arguably the *apeiron* was not a substance at all, for its only positive characteristic was potentiality. It was transformed into the four elements and thence into everything else, Anaximander said, by a process of eternal motion and ordering of elements governed by 'justice'. What he means by justice is intriguing, and the image he uses to describe its workings is that of a court of law:

> ... they [the opposing elements] give justice
> and reparation to one another for their injustice
> in accordance with the ordering of time.

However, this should not be taken to mean that the 'just' ordering of the universe is in any sense moral; the legal image is surely a metaphor drawn from the life of the city. What Anaximander seems to be suggesting is that the four elements came from the *apeiron* in equal measure and are held in balanced opposition to one another, and that something else – 'justice', which is

also related to time – is necessary to maintain or
continually redress the balance. Time never allows any
one of the elements to become permanently dominant,
hence the universe is in a constant process of change,
or alternation, for example in the seasons.

Perhaps springing from the notion of constant
change, Anaximander conceived of a process of
generation among animals that looks at first sight like a
distant ancestor of a theory of evolution. Viewed more
closely, his ideas about this process seem to owe more
to observation of the development of insects from
larvae: he is reported to have said that the first animals
were 'born in moisture, surrounded by prickly bark',
from which they later emerged on dry land, 'and for a
short time they lived a different kind of life'. Perhaps
having noticed that human young take much longer to
be able to feed or protect themselves than the young of
other animals, he posited the emergence of human
beings out of fish or fish-like creatures in a similar
process, 'not emerging and taking to the land until they
were able to fend for themselves'.

Anaximander is said to have been the first man to
make a map of the earth – which he conceived of as
cylindrical, set at the centre of a spherical universe
around which the sun, moon and stars circle,
equidistant from the earth, in a celestial wheel.
Anaximander uses the same image of something
bursting through a casing to describe the generation of
this world as he used for the emergence of animals:

> ... *something capable of generating hot and cold*
> *from the eternal was separated off at the genesis*

*of this world, and ... a sphere of flame grew
around the air surrounding the earth, like bark
round a tree. When this was torn off and closed
off into various circles, the sun and the moon and
the stars were constituted.*

He conceived of a series of wheels or hoops, set at
different distances from the earth, hollow and filled
with fire, and punctuated by openings or vents; light
or fire showing through these vents accounted for the
appearance of the heavenly bodies. The hoop of the sun
was twenty-seven times greater than the earth, that of
the moon eighteen times greater. Phases of the moon
and eclipses were explained in terms of the blocking
or opening of the vents. This picture may seem to us
extremely fanciful, but it contains two revolutionary
features: first, the notion that the universe was
spherical, and second, the idea that it was the circular
shape of the hoops that prevented them from falling in
towards the earth.

ANAXIMENES
(ACTIVE *c.* 546 BCE)

Anaximenes, the third in our 'succession' of early
Milesians, was a pupil or colleague of Anaximander.
However, he went back to Thales' idea that the
primordial stuff was an observable substance, choosing
air, and proposed that the single law that governed the
generation of matter was one of rarefaction and
condensation. Here was another process of continual
change and motion. The most rarefied condition of air
was fire; successive degrees of condensation produced

wind, clouds, water, earth and finally, at the densest,
stone. Rarefaction was caused by heating,
condensation by cooling. The movement involved in
rarefaction and condensation also made matter visible
or invisible.

On the shape of the universe, Anaximenes also
looked back to Thales: his earth, sun and other
heavenly objects were all fiery, shaped like flat discs
('the sun is flat like a leaf', says one fragment), and
airborne, turning in a circle above the flat earth. The
heavenly bodies would not fall through the air because,
being flat, they offered resistance. Anaximenes' model
of the universe and in particular the earth proved
highly influential: Anaxagoras and Democritus are
among those who agreed with him.

❱ Key Ideas of the Milesian Pioneers

- Thales, Anaximander and Anaximenes were the first materialist thinkers in Greece: they were concerned with the physical nature of the world about them and the universe, and sought an explanation of natural phenomena within the physical world itself.

- All three were *monists*: that is, they posited a single substance as the original, underlying, fundamental constitutive material of the universe. These were the first rationally argued attempts at reductionism, which seeks to explain things in the simplest possible terms. Whereas Thales and Anaximenes thought this primordial stuff was a naturally occurring substance, Anaximander suggested something different, a quality or potentiality he called *to apeiron* (the boundless).

- Though Thales did not take this step, Anaximander and Anaximenes both saw the universe as regulated – in Anaximander's case by cosmic justice, in Anaximenes' by the physical law of rarefaction and condensation.

- Although they disagreed on the nature of the primordial substance and the nature of the law that governed the universe, they shared a method of reasoned argument to support their hypotheses that they passed on to all their successors in Greece and that became a standard methodology for many centuries.

Chapter 4

Pythagoras
to Heraclitus

From harmony, from heavenly harmony,
This universal frame began ...
(John Dryden, *A song for St Cecilia's Day*, 1687)

With the next generation, philosophy began to spread out beyond Ionia. All three of the philosophers we shall meet in this chapter were born in Ionia, but both Pythagoras and Xenophanes ventured abroad while still young men. Xenophanes was itinerant for over sixty years, while Pythagoras and his followers settled in southern Italy, which then became the centre of Pythagoreanism in the fifth century BCE. The Pythagorean experiment was very different from the thinking of the Milesian pioneers, but with Xenophanes and Heraclitus, despite their differences, we are essentially back on the familiar ground of speculation about the nature and origin of the universe.

PYTHAGORAS AND HIS FOLLOWERS
(BORN *C.* 570 BCE)

Pythagoras is a classic case of how history can distort and falsify. Until about fifty years ago, everyone believed that 'Pythagoras' theorem' – the one about the square on the hypotenuse – had been discovered by a Greek mathematician called Pythagoras: not an unreasonable supposition. Then, in 1962, the great German classical scholar Walter Burkert cast into question nearly everything we thought we knew about Pythagoras. His researches showed that Pythagoras, as an individual, was not the 'father of mathematics', although there were mathematicians among his followers, and was almost certainly not personally the author of the famous theorem; it is not even entirely certain that he discovered the numerical ratio determining the intervals of the musical scale, another major discovery attributed to him. What did seem true was that he believed in the transmigration of souls and established a religious sect centred on that belief.

Legends grew up around Pythagoras while he was alive, and he was by far the most written-about of the Presocratics. His reputation as a mathematician could have been invented by Pythagoreans in southern Italy in the fifth century BCE and further boosted by subsequent writers. In any case, Pythagoreans' belief in reincarnation, their communal way of life, their secrecy, and their veneration of the founding figure make it difficult to identify individual members of Pythagoras' circle or to detect what is original to Pythagoras.

This misinformation in the sources may explain why there seem to be two very different Pythagorases: on the one hand the pioneering mathematician and researcher into the physics of music, on the other the charismatic mystic who believed in reincarnation and had a phobia about beans. That there was a man called Pythagoras is attested by a contemporary philosopher, Xenophanes (see page 59), who, according to Diogenes Laertius, tells a story – probably a joke at Pythagoras' expense – of Pythagoras' recognizing 'the soul of a dear friend' in the cries of a puppy as he passed by. But even this story is second-hand. The first direct reference to Pythagoras comes from Plato, and it is only a brief reference to the 'way of life' he established, not to his mathematical or philosophical achievements. Aristotle mentions these in some detail in his *Metaphysics*, but attributes them to 'the Pythagoreans'.

The historical Pythagoras was born probably about 570 BCE on the island of Samos. He gathered a circle of followers, including both men and women (highly unusual at the time), who lived a rigorously self-disciplined communal lifestyle organized around study, exercise and music. The community was religious, rule-bound and extremely secretive. Defection or revealing the secrets was punishable, even by death, according to several stories – another reason, perhaps, why we have no evidence of Pythagorean ideas before Plato.

Some time around 540–530 BCE, Pythagoras migrated with some followers to Croton in southern Italy (roughly, modern Calabria) and founded a community there, becoming influential and powerful in the city. But the Pythagoreans got on the wrong side of the citizens of Croton, were hounded out and moved on to Metapontum, where Pythagoras died, possibly violently. The region remained the centre of Pythagorean communities for a time, but their political ambitions seem to have caused their downfall: by the mid fourth century most of them had been violently destroyed and the survivors had fled to the Greek mainland.

Pythagoras marks the beginning of a different tradition of thought from that of the Milesians. He did not concern himself much with nature, being more interested in the soul and its qualities. He saw both the universe and the soul as endless and unchanging, the same things recurring eternally, and within this scheme the soul was subject to a series of reincarnations. It is not clear quite how he envisaged this, for he thought a soul could die after numerous reincarnations. He believed personal identity was preserved through incarnations, as in the story of the puppy, and one or two sources say that he remembered several past lives of his own. This would have been a very radical notion to Greeks brought up on Homer and the myths of Hades to explain what happened after death.

Pythagorean philosophy was full of mystical and religious thought. Much of it was expressed in short sayings or aphorisms, called *akousmata* (literally 'things heard'), which included the famous advice to abstain from beans but also statements about the universe, for example that the planets were bearers of divine vengeance ('the hounds of Persephone'), the purpose of thunder was to frighten souls in the underworld, and earthquakes were gatherings of the dead. Other *akousmata* took the form of instructions or prohibitions that seem frankly superstitious: 'Put on your right shoe first', 'Don't have children by a woman who wears gold', 'Don't look in a mirror by lamplight', and the like.

These are hardly scientific concepts – they are a good deal less scientific than those of the Ionian pioneers – and they make no use of reasoned argument at all. More interesting is the theory, combining the physical and the mystical aspects of Pythagorean thought, that the heavenly bodies moved in accordance with the same mathematical ratios that govern the concordant musical intervals, producing a harmony among the heavenly bodies. The sources make this one of the main Pythagorean ideas; it passed into much later literature as a popular poetic image, the 'music of the spheres'. But in the end it could not be sustained. The reason is ironic: 'Pythagoras' theorem' turned out to disprove all the Pythagoreans' other ideas about number and its role in the universe.

The Pythagoreans had speculated that everything in the world, and the relations between things, could be expressed in terms of numbers. This meant not just assigning a number to each thing, but saying that all things *were* numbers. Their attempt to establish measurability combined the intellectual and the mystical in a way that seems strange to us: they thought, for instance, that 'marriage is five' because it joins the first even (female, limited) number with the first odd (male, unlimited) one. Even the soul had a number.

Their concept of number was not just arithmetical but geometrical: they conceived of numbers spatially, as arrangements of points laid out on a surface (there is an echo of this conception today when we speak of numbers being squared or cubed). The square numbers were 4, 9, 16 and so on, the triangular numbers 3, 6, 10, and so on. Justice was four, the first square number. Ten, a triangular number made up of 1 + 2 + 3 + 4, was particularly important.

In particular, the Pythagoreans had noticed that musical intervals could be expressed numerically, related to the lengths of strings on a lyre. From this discovery they postulated that if musical harmony depended on numerical ratios, the harmony of the universe (an idea related to Anaximander's balance) could also be expressed numerically, and they developed a system for this.

However, these conclusions could only be arrived at by using whole numbers. What 'Pythagoras' theorem' proved was that there was a general universal relationship holding for all possible right-angled triangles – namely that for all right-angled triangles the length of any hypotenuse when squared was equal to the sum of the squared lengths of the other two sides. But the theorem worked with sides whose lengths were measurable in whole numbers only sometimes, whereas, in practice, the sides of right-angled triangles could be of any length. When, for example, the two shorter sides of the triangle were 3 and 4 units long, the hypotenuse came out neatly at 5. But if a triangle with two equal sides 1 unit long was used, the result obtained by applying the theorem, while obviously bigger than the two 1-unit sides, was bigger in a proportion that they could not express numerically or even recognize as a number – the 'square root of 2'. They could draw this hypotenuse, but they could not measure it in a way that made sense within their numbering system. They had discovered what mathematicians call 'incommensurable' lengths and irrational numbers, but these discoveries, while immensely important mathematically, brought their whole numerically based cosmology crashing down.

In the fifth century BCE Pythagoras' successors split into two factions, Aphorists (*akousmatikoi*) and Mathematicians (*mathematikoi*), reflecting the two sides of Pythagorean thought. It seems most likely that the bulk of the mathematical and astronomical theory attributed to Pythagoras emanated from the latter group. **Hippasus** of Croton was said to have been the first of the Mathematicians; he is credited with the discovery of the harmonic mean. The first fully-fledged Pythagorean mathematician of whom we have real evidence is **Archytas** of Tarentum, a contemporary of Plato highly regarded in antiquity, who made important discoveries in geometry and harmonics. But apart from Archytas and another fifth-century BCE Pythagorean, **Philolaus**, true mathematics in Greece was advanced by a completely different series of thinkers. It was the mystical tradition represented by the Aphorists that became influential, most importantly to Plato, and after him to a long tradition of Platonist philosophers right up to the Middle Ages.

XENOPHANES

(c. 580–c. 480 BCE)

Meanwhile, the poet and philosopher Xenophanes of Colophon was carrying the Ionian intellectual enlightenment westward from Asia Minor. He left his native city at the age of twenty-five, and seems to have spent the rest of his long life travelling around Greece and Sicily as a jobbing poet. Many of his verses were satirical and it is surprising that his unorthodox views didn't get him into trouble. He wrote on Pythagoras and other early philosophers – it is to him that we owe the story of Pythagoras and the puppy – but he also had his own ideas about the physical world, though he did not express them systematically in a work devoted to the subject.

Xenophanes was the first philosopher of religion. He was extremely critical of the traditional portrayal of the gods in Homer and the epic poems, where they behaved so disappointingly like humans, forever committing 'theft and adultery and mutual deception'. This doesn't mean that Xenophanes was an atheist; on the contrary, he could be very pious. His remarks are a critical analysis of religion as it was practised in his day. He believed that people imagined gods in their own image:

> But mortals think that gods are born,
> and have clothes and speech and shape like
> their own ...
> But if cows and horses or lions had hands ...
> then horses would draw the forms of gods like
> horses, cows like cows, and each would make
> their bodies similar in shape to their own.
> (Xenophanes, in Clement of Alexandria, Miscellanies V)

People of different races would even give their gods features just like their own: Ethiopians would make them dark-skinned, while Thracians would make them blue-eyed and ginger-haired. Xenophanes seems in these verses to have been talking about the limits to human knowledge: he was not simply saying that people are stupid or gullible or misled, but was putting forward a much more serious idea: that humans *cannot* understand gods or the divine; we can only try to understand them by imagining that they are like us and share our faults and frailties.

Xenophanes hypothesized instead a non-mythological theology centred on a single or supreme god – it is not entirely clear from the surviving fragments whether he is referring to just one god or a god that is the greatest of many. The important thing is that this divinity is not a person but an abstract, impersonal divine principle, 'similar to mortals neither in shape nor in thought', able to 'shake all things' by the force of its mind alone, capable of accomplishing everything while always reposing in the same state or place – and ultimately unknowable to human minds.

He applied the same demythification to a number of natural phenomena which in Homeric and Hesiodic poems were gods and goddesses: for instance Iris, the rainbow, who to the epic poets (and most sixth-century Greeks) was the messenger goddess as well as the rainbow, was in Xenophanes' account just a multi-coloured cloud, beautiful but not divine. In this he can be seen as carrying on the same rational approach to the universe as the previous generation of Milesians; and indeed he had his own theory of the fundamental primary substance, which he may have defined as earth or water, or a mixture of the two, depending on which source you are reading.

In meteorology, he made the remarkably prescient observation that clouds are formed by vaporization caused by the heat of the sun, and used this concept to suggest explanations for a number of astronomical phenomena. In short, Xenophanes combined a new approach to belief in a divine order with the lively enquiry into the nature of the world and its contents typical of his Ionian predecessors.

HERACLITUS

(540–475 BCE)

'Heraclitus, having pity and compassion for our [human] condition, constantly wore a sorrowful face, his eyes brimming with tears', said Montaigne of this most enigmatic representative of the Ionian school. Nicknamed 'the Weeping Philosopher' very early on, he was paired with Democritus, who was dubbed 'the Laughing Philosopher'. He was also known, even in his own lifetime, as 'the Riddler', or 'the Obscure' – with good reason, for his philosophy is full of cryptic utterances.

Not much is known about his life except that he was born in Ephesus (modern Efes, in Turkey) into an aristocratic, possibly royal, family, and that he wrote a book on nature. Of course that book has not survived, and because of his obscure style, his love of wordplay, his complex ideas and the many and various interpretations to which they have been subjected, it is particularly difficult to see what he is getting at.

However, we can tease out a few of his ideas. He carried on the Milesian tradition, especially in his model of the universe, but, like the Pythagoreans, he also had an interest in the soul and the afterlife and in human knowledge.

A central Heraclitean idea is one we shall find familiar from Anaximander, that the natural universe is governed by a law of opposites held in tension: '… what is at variance agrees with itself; it is an attunement of opposite tensions, as in the bow and the lyre'. In general, he saw the universe as made up of pairs of opposites in contention or 'strife': what keeps them in existence is the 'justice' that keeps the opposites in tension – another Anaximandrian idea, but with the difference that Heraclitus saw justice and strife as themselves necessary, overarching opposites and the balanced tension between other pairs of opposites as eternally present, maintained by that between justice and strife.

This essential, but paradoxical, unity of opposites is very prominent in Heraclitus' thought and is expressed in many images, for example: 'The sea is most pure and polluted water: for fish, it is drinkable and preserves life; for men, it is undrinkable and it kills'; or one of his most famous riddles, 'The path up and down is one and the same'. This assertion has been variously understood. On the one hand, it may be an image from daily life illustrating the unity of opposites by the fact that the same road can appear in two opposite ways, depending on which direction you are looking along it; it tells us that the natures of things are not absolute in themselves but relative to our point of view. On the other hand, it appears as a more complex metaphor referring to the process of cyclical change by which the cosmos eternally comes into being.

Fire was the element Heraclitus chose as the primordial substance – or rather the primordial process – of the world. He maintained more firmly than his Ionian predecessors that the world had always existed and had been made 'neither by god nor man, but always was, is and will be, an ever-living fire, kindling and being quenched in proportion'. Everything else had arisen from this eternally ongoing process of combustion. Linking this with the principle of balanced opposition, Heraclitus seems to have conceived of the universe as an everlasting and ever-changing modification of fire, with the things in it each kept in existence by the balanced tension between justice and strife. From this process a universal harmony emerged.

This brings us to the question of change. In contrast to the radical idea of oneness and stasis being put forward around the same time by his Eleatic contemporary Parmenides (see chapter 5), Heraclitus claimed that 'everything changes and nothing remains'. Since we are dealing with Heraclitus, this is not as simple as it looks, but suggests a more complex theory, with Milesian overtones, of time, matter and change: 'We both step and do not step in the same rivers ... We both are and are not.' Change is the constant fact of the universe, and everything is always partway between being what it just was and what it will be next, in a process of momentaneous generation and dissolution. We both are what we are now and are not what we were a nanosecond ago or will be a nanosecond in the future. And in the transformation there is a point at which we are all three.

Like Xenophanes, Heraclitus rejected the accepted Greek religion but believed in the existence of something divine, which he identified with the eternal cosmic fire. But there was also another principle, much debated by scholars up to today, which Heraclitus called *logos*. This is a word with many meanings: the basic meaning is 'word'; it can also mean 'reason' or 'account', and has connotations of planning, measurement, proportion. Heraclitus uses it to refer to the rational principle governing the law of change and the unity of opposites. The process of change is the *logos* – the logic or rationale – of the universe. Opinions are divided as to the relation between the *logos* and the divine (*theos*), and Heraclitus himself does not make the distinction clear.

Heraclitus is emphatic on the imperfection of human knowledge: 'Men do not understand the things they meet with – not even when they have learned them do they know them.' In particular, most divine acts escape our knowledge. The individual's subjective knowledge is incomplete, and wisdom lies not in learning but in the soul's awakening to the *logos*: 'wisdom is one thing: to grasp the knowledge of how all things are steered through all.' This is the wisdom to which the philosopher aspires.

Heraclitus had enormous influence on Plato, Aristotle, the Stoics and the early Christians. Interpretations of his work have been many and varied over the centuries, and philosophers are still discussing what he might have meant. His theories have been considered as (admittedly distant) precursors of the laws of conservation and energy; his ideas about the divine *logos* found their way, via Plato, into Christian theology. It may not be too great a stretch of the imagination to suggest that the opening words of the gospel of John – 'In the beginning was the Word, and the Word was with God, and the Word was God' – may echo this *logos*, reaching right back to Heraclitus.

» Key Ideas

- **Pythagoreans:** Developed two broad strands of thought, one rational, one mystical. The former gave rise to important discoveries about mathematics and the mathematics of music; the latter developed a religion based on communal life and ruled by a series of precepts or aphorisms. Pythagoras himself was almost certainly not responsible for 'Pythagoras' theorem' or the idea of the harmony of the heavenly bodies, but was the founder of the religious sect.

- **Xenophanes:** Criticized orthodox representations of the gods and proposed a divinity that was abstract, impersonal, all-powerful but unmoving and ultimately unknowable to humans.

- **Heraclitus:** The fundamental process of the universe is eternal fire, which is divine. The universe and matter itself are constantly changing but are kept in existence in a balanced tension of opposites. A universal harmony emerges from the conflict, produced by this constant dissolution and formation. The whole universe is governed by *logos* and god. Ordinary human knowledge cannot comprehend this.

Chapter 5

The Thinkers from Elea

Parmenides stands beside [Heraclitus] as counter-image, likewise expressing a type of truth-teller but one formed of ice rather than fire, pouring cold piercing light all around.

(Nietzsche, *Philosophie im tragischen Zeitalter der Griechen* [*Philosophy in the Tragic Age of the Greeks*], 1873)

Roughly contemporary with Heraclitus, in the south Italian city of Elea, a different kind of metaphysics was being developed by Parmenides. It was continued by Zeno of Elea and, somewhat later, by Melissus. These philosophers used logic in a new way. What we particularly notice about them is that they moved away from deduction based on empirical observation and argued at a highly abstract level. Few if any of their ideas had much to do with what we see around us in the natural world – indeed Parmenides argued that the evidence of our senses is always false. He developed and taught a theory of oneness that held that change and motion are impossible. Zeno tested – and eventually produced arguments to confirm – the idea that motion is illusory, illustrating the gap between strict logical deduction and common sense, in a series of paradoxes, some of which are still familiar to us, for example that of Achilles and the tortoise (see page 74).

PARMENIDES

(BORN POSSIBLY *c.* 515 BCE)

Parmenides was an aristocratic citizen of Elea and a legislator as well as a philosopher. Plato named one of his late dialogues after him, setting the discussion during a visit Parmenides made to Athens when he was about sixty-five, together with the much younger Zeno, to meet the young Socrates. This would make him a somewhat younger contemporary of Heraclitus, some of whose arguments he appears to counter.

Parmenides may have been a student of Xenophanes; according to Diogenes Laertius, he did not follow his teachings, but his assertion that all things are one can be seen as an extension of Xenophanes' concept of a single, unknowable, impersonal god who 'abides in the same place, unmoving', a concept ultimately traceable back to the Ionian idea of a single primordial substance.

His ideas have come down to us in the form of a didactic poem of which eighteen fragments are quoted in a commentary on Aristotle by the sixth-century CE scholar Simplicius. It was composed in two parts called *The Way of Truth* and *The Way of Opinion* (also translated as *The Way of Seeming*). Most of the surviving text is from the former. Here he developed his extraordinary theory of oneness. By relating existence itself to thinking about existence, and thinking about non-existence or non-existent things, he deduced that everything that exists ('what is') must be 'ungenerated and indestructible, whole, of one kind and unwavering', spatially and temporally continuous, and unchanging – but also finite, in fact spherical. Given the high level of abstraction at which Parmenides was working, the spherical shape seems an oddly concrete detail; but Parmenides explains that only in a sphere is every point on the surface equidistant from the centre.

Despite the evidence of our senses, our material world of plurality and change is a 'false and deceitful' illusion, and any belief in it is mistaken. The only true being is the One – which is not a unity of opposites such as Heraclitus posited, but a concept of ultimate reality (Being, or 'what is') that embodies absolute stasis.

Parmenides arrived at this startling conclusion by a process of extremely abstract logical argument deliberately divorced from empirical investigation; he used what the nineteenth-century German philosopher Nietzsche (1844–1900) called 'the rope ladder of logic' to arrive at metaphysical conclusions that follow logically but are completely contrary to anything we can perceive empirically. When Parmenides argues, for instance, that 'being' is eternal, he is reasoning that besides what is real there is *nothing whatsoever*; so what could have brought 'reality' into being? It doesn't make sense to say that 'nothing did', so if it weren't always there it could never be – but of course there *is* reality ('what is'), and logically it must therefore be eternal.

Some late-nineteenth-century scholars considered Parmenides the discoverer of logic, partly because his poem contains the first known use of the word *logos* to signify rational discourse or argument. Bernard Russell's modification of this view in 1946, in which he says that what Parmenides really invented was 'a metaphysics based on logic', is perhaps a more astute assessment.

Another problem in the poem is that of the relationship between knowledge, belief and thought. However, Parmenides' apparent conflation of the existence of something and knowledge or thinking about it contributes to the difficulty of understanding him. He thought that knowledge could apply only to the One; opinion was the unreliable kind of perception that ordinary people had about the material world:

> ... the road along which mortals who know
> nothing wander, two-headed ...
> And they are carried along both deaf and blind,
> bewildered, undiscerning crowds, by whom
> to be and not to be are deemed the same
> and not the same ...

This distinction between knowledge (of the One) and belief or opinion (with respect to the illusory sensible world) is of course the basis on which the whole poem is structured. But it is also one that was developed more fully by Plato in his theory of Forms (see chapter 9).

In the second part of his poem, *The Way of Opinion*, Parmenides included material relating to the real world, some of which is actually true. For instance, he was the first Greek to propose that the earth is spherical, and that the light of the moon is reflected. But the discovery is undermined by the fact that he included it in the part of his poem that described what he thought false, not part of the Way of Truth. Did he, then, think these discoveries worthless? If so, why publish them? Scholars have debated this ever since. Nietzsche thought he had simply changed his whole approach at some point in his career: 'Once in his life', he surmised, 'Parmenides, probably at a fairly advanced age, had a moment of purest, absolutely bloodless abstraction, unclouded by any reality.' But the opening lines of *The Way of Opinion* seem to follow on from *The Way of Truth* so directly that it is difficult to imagine that they were written at a different time – and particularly that they were written *before* Parmenides' moment of enlightenment:

> Here I cease for you the warranted account and thought about the truth. Henceforward learn mortal opinions, listening to the deceitful arrangements of my words.

Parmenides seems to have wanted to have his cake and eat it too; or perhaps, having produced in *The Way of Truth* a conclusion that looked implausible however logically arrived at, he was offering as well a more conventional account of the world that people might understand.

The poem also has an intriguing prologue, couched in allegorical terms rather different from the style of the rest. In it he tells how he came to write the poem. The daughters of the Sun brought him in a chariot to a region 'beyond the tread of men' to the gates of the paths of

Night and Day, to which 'punitive Justice holds the keys'. Justice is persuaded to open the gates, and beyond them he is greeted by a goddess who tells him he has been sent to her by Right and Justice and that he must

> ... learn all things, both the unwavering heart of well-rounded [or persuasive – sources vary] truth and the opinions of mortals in which there is no true warranty.

'Truth' here refers to the theory of oneness described in the first part of the poem, 'opinion' to the 'illusory' world described in the second.

But there is more about justice. In *The Way of Truth*, Justice appears again in a new guise, together with Necessity and Fate, making up the triad of forces that hold 'what is' firmly in place and ensure its constancy: 'Justice does not loosen her fetters so far as to allow it [Being, or 'what is'] to come into being or to pass away, but holds it fast.' Necessity and Fate also hold it 'enchained' and 'fettered'; the image of coercion and binding is very strong and is applied to all three forces. Here is a personalization of abstract entities, and a mythologizing, not to say mystical, language that seems closer to Orphism than to the rope ladder of logic. The presence of justice and necessity in Parmenides' account also suggests that he believed in a moral force operating on 'what is'. To quote Shirley Darcus Sullivan, 'Justice makes Being what it is: one.'

Parmenides' poem is extremely strange. It is difficult to see why he bothered to write the second part if he thought the conclusions of the first part true, yet it seems to have been part of the composition from the outset. Then there are the many obscurities of *The Way of Truth* in both content and style. Aristotle himself, in his treatise *On Generation and Corruption*, thought the central tenets 'close to madness'. None the less, filtered through Plato, this became one of the most influential works of ancient Greek philosophy.

MELISSUS
(FL. 440s BCE)

A generation or two after Parmenides, Melissus, a citizen of Samos but intellectually an Eleatic, recast Parmenides' opaque verses in prose. His version, of which some sizeable fragments are preserved and paraphrased by Simplicius, is certainly easier to read than Parmenides' original, though rather repetitive. Although he reiterated Parmenides' positions for the most part, sometimes producing new supporting arguments, he disagreed with him on a few key points. He was particularly concerned to clarify Parmenides' thesis that 'what is' is one; and in the interests of this he reasoned against Parmenides that the universe must be spatially infinite, not a finite sphere, thus doing away with one of the apparent inconsistencies of Parmenides' central concept. He also adduced a quite detailed argument to support the idea, which Parmenides had simply asserted, that the world of the senses is illusory:

> ... there are many things with form and strength, but they all seem to us to alter and to change from what they were each time they were seen. So it is clear that we do not see correctly ... if there exist many things, they must be such as the one thing is.

However, like Parmenides, he finds it possible to reconcile what we perceive with the senses with the Parmenidean stasis only by denying that common sense is valid.

By Melissus' time, both Empedocles and the Atomists, whom we shall meet in the next chapter, had advanced alternatives to Parmenides' strict monism; Melissus' work can be seen as a determined attempt to defend Parmenides' notion of the universe against these newer ideas.

ZENO

(BORN C. 490 BCE)

A friend and student of Parmenides, Zeno is best known for his series of logical paradoxes, which illustrate the method of *reductio ad absurdum* – proving or disproving a statement by taking its consequences through strictly logical steps to the point of absurdity. Zeno was the first to use this method, which has become a standard topic in the study of logic. He seems not to have produced a philosophical theory of his own, but to have devoted himself to creating logical arguments of this kind in response to the theories of others and in particular in support of Parmenides.

According to Plato in the *Parmenides*, the dialogue in which he makes Parmenides and Zeno participants, Zeno created these arguments to support Parmenides' view against those of his philosophical opponents who aimed to refute his strict monism. However, Zeno doesn't simply say that Parmenides is right and his opponents are wrong. Rather, he designs some forty arguments to show that it is just as paradoxical to assume the existence of plurality as it is to assume that there is only oneness. Plato has Zeno reply to Socrates:

My book [aims] to show that [the anti-Parmenidean] hypothesis – that more things than one exist – leads to even more ridiculous results, if you examine it properly, than the hypothesis that only one thing exists.

The most famous of the paradoxes are four arguments proving the impossibility of motion, apparently supporting Parmenides' idea that motion was illusory. The set of arguments was systematically planned to confront anti-Parmenideans with a complex destructive dilemma. All four paradoxes are described by Aristotle in the sixth book of his *Physics*. Here are the three familiar ones (the fourth, concerning the movement of people in opposite directions in a space, is less well known).

Achilles and the tortoise
Aristotle set out the problem as follows: 'In a race, the fastest runner can never overtake the slowest, for the pursuer must first reach the point whence the pursued set out, so that the slower one must always be in the lead.' Imagine the Greek epic hero Achilles, famed for his speed, in a race with a humble tortoise. If the tortoise, as the slower contestant, is given a head start, it will always remain ahead; for by the time Achilles has reached the point from which the tortoise started out, the tortoise has moved on – by a shorter distance than Achilles has covered, admittedly, but still it has

moved on. And whenever Achilles reaches a point that the tortoise has just left, it is still ahead. Since there is an infinite number of points Achilles has to reach where the tortoise has already been, he will never catch up, for even though the distance between the racers becomes infinitesimal, it can never shrink to nothing. Hence, Zeno argues, motion is impossible.

The paradox of dichotomy, or halving
This paradox says that if something is divisible, theoretically it can be cut in two an infinite number of times, until it either becomes an infinite number of infinitesimal pieces from which the whole could be reconstituted, or else disappears into nothing, which would mean that the whole thing was constituted from nothing – which is impossible. Therefore, Zeno concludes, there cannot be a plurality of things but just the one. Aristotle saw this paradox as a variation on 'Achilles and the tortoise', but there is a further problem in it, illustrated by the case of Achilles and the racetrack, or indeed anyone progressing from point A to point B. There is no competitor this time, but to get to the end of the track – from A to B – you have to reach the halfway mark; before you can get there, you have to get a quarter of the way there; before that, an eighth of the way … and so on till, in the end, with infinitesimal divisions of the distance, it will take you for ever just to start off.

The flight of the arrow
This paradox applies the same principle as the dichotomy to time as well as distance. The assumption is that the time it takes for a flying arrow to reach its

target can be divided into instants, an instant being defined as an indivisibly small amount of time. If the arrow moves during an instant, it would have to be at one place at the beginning of the instant and another at the end. But since the instant is indivisible, it has no beginning or end; therefore the arrow cannot move through that instant, or any other, and so it will never move, showing again that motion is impossible.

The dilemma here is that either reality (as represented by space, distances, time) is infinitely divisible or it is not (in which case there are ultimate indivisible particles – sizes, lengths, moments). If you choose the first alternative, you have to face the consequences of the Achilles paradoxes; but if you choose the second, you have to face the consequences of the Arrow paradox. Either way the consequences are unacceptable, and the advocates of change and motion are stymied.

Of course, all these paradoxes go against any notion of common sense and sense perception. Zeno argued that you could get round them by dismissing the very idea of divisibility – that is, by subscribing wholesale to Parmenides' monism. But they can also be solved by taking motion, time, and space not as consisting of an infinite number of points but as each being a continuum. Even Aristotle seems to recognize this; and modern mathematics shows us that it is perfectly possible for space or time to be infinitely divisible in any case. Zeno's achievement, in the end, lies more in the method than the matter.

» Key Ideas

- **Parmenides:** Used logical argument to prove that being, or 'what is', is single, without beginning or end, continuous, and also finite and spherical; and that, contrary to the evidence of our senses, our belief in plurality and change in the world is erroneous and the material word around us is an illusion.

- **Melissus:** In a prose version of Parmenides' work, generally supported Parmenides' positions and provided some arguments of his own to strengthen them, disagreeing in points of detail in order to strengthen the central thesis of oneness.

- **Zeno:** Rather than coming up with a metaphysical system of his own, devoted his attention to devising paradoxes supporting Parmenides' monism, for instance by showing that movement is illusory.

Chapter 6

Pluralists and Atomists

> *Soul of the world! Inspir'd by thee,*
> *the jarring Seeds of Matter did agree.*
> *Thou didst the scatter'd Atoms bind ...*
>
> (Nicholas Brady, libretto of Henry Purcell,
> *Hail! Bright Cecilia*, 1692)

All the early Presocratic theories contending that the world is made up of just one primary substance are *monistic* theories. But the contradiction between theory and common sense and empiricism that culminated in the extreme monism of Parmenides must have become a source of frustration. We know that by the time of Zeno arguments were being produced to counter those of Parmenides, since it was just such arguments that Zeno wanted to scotch. From about Zeno's time, then, Greek philosophers began to advance *pluralist* theories about the nature of the universe, speculating that it is made up not of one kind of matter, but of many. A third tendency in Presocratic philosophy did not utterly reject Parmenides, but attempted to reconcile his arguments with reasoning that took some account of perceptible reality. The variety of theories advanced by these men, as well as the subjects addressed, are evidence of the remarkable intellectual vigour of the mid fifth century BCE in Greece, even, as we have seen, in the midst of constant war and political upheaval across the Greek world.

Important philosophers propounding pluralist solutions in this period are Empedocles, Anaxagoras, and the Atomists Leucippus and Democritus.

Pluralist Theories

EMPEDOCLES
(c. 493–c. 433 BCE)

Empedocles is one of the most colourful figures we know of in ancient Greece. A Sicilian patrician, from the city of Acragas, he was a philosopher, a prophet, an orator and a statesman, and at the same time a mystic, a self-proclaimed miracle-worker and healer, who also claimed to be a god. Not altogether surprisingly, he was exiled for his political activities in the seesaw between democracy and tyranny common within many Greek cities at the time. He was well connected and said to have been acquainted with many of his contemporary philosophers. Fantastical stories grew up around him, as around Pythagoras, for instance that he died by jumping into the volcano Etna to prove he was a god. (According to the story, Etna regurgitated one of his shoes, to prove he was not.)

Like other Presocratic thinkers, Empedocles was involved in both philosophical speculation and religious activity. He wrote two poems, which broadly cover his theories about the natural world and its origins and religious questions respectively. Two of several contributions attributed to him in natural philosophy are the discovery that air is a distinct substance – he observed that when a vessel is placed upside down in water some of the air in it remains inside, separate from the water flowing in – and an observation of centrifugal force, noticing that when you whirl a bucket of water round on the end of a string, the water stays inside it.

Empedocles' cosmology provided the first pluralistic answer to Parmenides. He took from Parmenides the idea that the universe is spherical and everlasting, but disagreed that it is motionless and changeless; he returned to the idea, hinted at by Heraclitus, of endless change, which he hypothesizes as cyclical alternation. He concluded that reality must be completely full, a totality containing no gaps. Though constantly moving, things do not move into or out of empty space but exchange places with each other within the closed system of the sphere: the totality or *plenum* remains unchanged as a whole, while the parts replace one another within it.

Empedocles proposed that all matter is made up of four elements or 'roots': water, earth, air and fire. These are eternal and equally proportioned in the universe, and combine or separate in the processes of generation and destruction. The idea of four elements is not completely original with Empedocles, though its centrality in the cosmology is: Anaximander had mentioned the four elements before him but had proposed a more fundamental primary substance, the *apeiron* (see chapter 3). But the system of four basic elements proved remarkably persistent: it was still being used for classification, by doctors and others, in the seventeenth century.

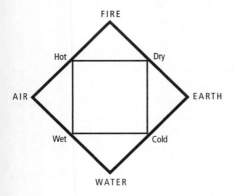

Empedocles' four elements were related to four qualities, of which each element possessed two. Thus, fire was hot and dry, air hot and moist, water moist and cold, and earth cold and dry. All matter consisted of different combinations of these.

Empedocles added to the four elements two opposing forces (or possibly substances) that operate upon them: Love, causing attraction between different forms of matter, and Strife, causing repulsion and their separation. These ideas hark back to Heraclitus' notions of strife and justice producing balance; but in Empedocles' system the fluctuation of the universe is cyclical and eternal, an endless, reiterative tussle in which sometimes Love, sometimes Strife, is dominant. Under the influence of Love, all the elements join together, forming the world sphere at one extreme of the alternation; when it is the turn of Strife the sphere falls apart and its elements are separated into distinct, concentric masses of fire, air, earth and water, with earth at the centre and fire at the periphery. Then the process reverses, and the Sphere is re-formed. The movement of the universe is imagined as 'whirling' in a vortex, with Love and Strife alternately reaching the centre, where they are dominant, and travelling outward again. This system is not unproblematic. The surviving texts are not clear, and there are still divergent interpretations of the workings of these processes.

Empedocles' speculations embraced a theory about the formation of animals and plants that hints obscurely at evolution. He described a series of generations in which increasingly finished forms of life appeared. In the first two generations, many of the creatures were monstrous or fragmentary:

Naked arms wandered, devoid of shoulders,
and eyes strayed alone, begging for foreheads,
and later, men were born double-headed and
double-chested – man-faced oxen arose, and
again ox-headed men ...

The third generations produced 'whole-natured forms' arising from the earth, but not yet human, having 'as yet no desirable shape to their members, nor any voice ... native to man'. The fourth generations are those that produced our world – a world about which Empedocles suddenly takes a rather pessimistic view, remarking that birth in itself is traumatic and leads only to death.

The sequence of generations appears to be occurring within the larger pattern of change, the alternating dominance of Love and Strife in the world vortex.

Exactly how the zoogony (the creation of life forms) is related to the cosmogony (the creation of the universe) is also still debated, especially in the light of recently discovered fragments of Empedocles' work, but the important underlying idea is that the varying combinations of elements generates different substances – for instance that approximately equal parts of earth, water, air and fire combine to make flesh and blood, and that they are present in different proportions in bone.

It is in the religious part of Empedocles' work that he makes claims to divinity or at the very least superior wisdom. His ideas here have Pythagorean resonances, in particular as regards the transmigration of souls. He gives a more explicit moral underpinning to this than Pythagoras does: echoing the biblical story of the fall of Lucifer and the angels, he describes the fall from grace of 'spirits who enjoyed a life of bliss' but who erred and were condemned to a sequence of mortal incarnations as humans, animals and even plants. Empedocles sees himself as one of these souls, 'an exile from the gods and a wanderer'.

Among other pieces of advice reminiscent of the Pythagoreans, Empedocles recommends vegetarianism and not killing living things:

> *Will you not cease from harsh-sounding slaughter? Do you not see*
> *That it is one another you devour in the carelessness of your thought?*

In other words, 'don't eat that meat; you don't know who it's been.'

ANAXAGORAS

(c. 500–c. 428 BCE)

Born in Clazomenae in Ionia, Anaxagoras was the first
Greek philosopher actually to live in Athens, where he
arrived in about 480, possibly with the Persian army of
Xerxes. He is said to have stayed there for about thirty
years and was a friend of the Athenian leader Pericles.
This was his downfall, however, for he fell foul of
Pericles' enemies and was forced to flee the city. He
spent the rest of his life in Lampsacus, where he
founded a school.

Although Anaxagoras was a few years older than
Empedocles, he followed him in several respects,
notably in the belief that motion and hence change are
possible. His ideas also have some resemblances to
those of his contemporaries Leucippus and
Democritus.

A number of aspects of Anaxagoras' model of the
world are problematic and are still debated. However,
it is possible to outline its main features. Anaxagoras
combines ideas influenced by the Milesian tradition
carried on by Xenophanes and Heraclitus, and Eleatic
arguments deriving from Parmenides concerning the
proper logical process of argument and deduction into
these questions. His arguments are therefore
conducted at a highly theoretical level. He also
accepted Parmenides' argument that generation and
destruction of the fundamental matter are impossible,
and he explained apparent changes of this kind by
mixture and separation of constitutive ingredients:

... nothing comes to be or passes away, but is mixed together and dissociated from the things that are.

Generation and destruction are thus merely rearrangements of the ingredients. Growth and nutrition, for instance, happen without qualitative change, with only changes in the proportion of ingredients. Eating causes no qualitative change in either the eater or the thing eaten, but merely an addition of the ingredients in the food to those in the eater, changing their proportions and thus the characteristics (such as size) of the eater.

Anaxagoras was a quite radical pluralist, positing a universe containing not just four fundamental elements but one composed of, or filled with, a limitless number of ingredients, which he called 'seeds', making up an infinitely complex matter. There are seeds of every distinct kind of matter or substance occurring in nature – metals, wood, etc. – including qualities, conceived as materials – the hot, the cold, the dry, the dark, and so on. However, no substance or quality is pure: everything contains a mixture of all the ingredients that exist; every ingredient is everywhere, always. Every seed contains a portion of every other. Unsurprisingly, this assertion has been the subject of many interpretations and much debate. Anaxagoras' explanation was that things are infinitely divisible – another of his axioms was that there is no limit to smallness. So, with a definite nod in the direction of Zeno's dichotomy, Anaxagoras argued that in the division and subdivision of the ingredients in any substance, there can be infinitely small parts of all the other substances, but never none. Thus there is no such thing as an entirely pure substance: substances are distinguished in ordinary life by their predominant substance or quality, but they still contain admixtures of all the other substances or qualities, even if those are infinitesimal. The way in which they are mixed is also interesting: the 'everything-in-everything' mixture is not like plant seeds in a packet, or a bag of hundreds and thousands, but seems to involve a kind of inter-penetration that is closer to chemical combination.

The only thing that is entirely unmixed is *Nous* (Mind or Thought). It is 'limitless and independent, and it has been mixed with no thing but is alone by itself'. It is also 'the finest of all things and the purest, and it possesses all knowledge about everything, and it has the greatest strength'. *Nous* is also the original force that set the world in motion. Being different from everything else it also was able to move other things. 'All things were together. Then Thought came and arranged them.' Although Anaxagoras thought that every substance is eternal, he also held that there had been a beginning, in which everything was present in an unlimited (*apeiron*), undifferentiated mass. The cosmos formed when *Nous* set in motion a rotation that gradually spread from 'a little region' to a wider revolution, separating out the seeds of matter, 'the dense from the rare, and the hot from the cold, and the bright from the dark .... And there are many portions of many things, but nothing completely separates off or dissociates one from another except thought.'

The sun, moon, air and aether are also seen as having separated off in this rotation. The concept of *Nous* is one of Anaxagoras' most innovative ideas; but we cannot tell on the basis of the surviving fragments of his work whether he conceived of *Nous* as an intelligent designer of the universe or not.

Anaxagoras' cosmology is complex but elegant, and its working out is relatively comprehensible. He was highly esteemed in antiquity, but his theory of the universe was not, in the end, influential. It was overtaken by the theories of the Atomists, though it must have influenced them at least.

The Atomists

We tend to yoke together the Atomist philosophers, **Leucippus** and **Democritus**, like Laurel and Hardy or, more appropriately perhaps, Crick and Watson, the discoverers of the structure of DNA. Greek historians of philosophy did so too, so much so that it is hard for us to identify the specific contribution of each, though there is a rough consensus that Leucippus was the 'inventor' or originator of atomism and his student Democritus was responsible for the detailed working out of the theory. We cannot be sure exactly how – or even where – they collaborated, since the evidence that Leucippus ever visited or settled in Abdera on the Thracian coast, where Democritus lived, is debatable, and any evidence that Democritus ever visited Leucippus in his home city is absent.

In fact we know practically nothing about Leucippus;
even his birthplace is disputed. It was probably Miletus,
though it may have been Elea. He was active around
440 BCE, but we do not know his dates of birth or death.
Simplicius said that he had 'something in common'
with Parmenides but took a contrary path to those of
Parmenides and Xenophanes about 'what exists'.

We know a little more about the long-lived and
immensely learned Democritus (*c.* 460–*c.* 370 BCE). He
was probably the most prolific Greek philosopher after
Aristotle (who thought highly of his work), and the
disappearance of the vast majority of his writings is a
great loss. He wrote on ethical subjects (contentment,
manliness or virtue, wisdom); on natural science (a vast
range of topics ranging from a description of the whole
world to treatises on flavours and colours); on various
natural phenomena such as the heavens, the atmosphere,
fire, sounds, plants and animals; on mathematics,
literature, medicine and even farming. He acquired the
nickname of 'the Laughing Philosopher' – and in later
ages was often paired with the 'weeping' Heraclitus –
because he set great value on cheerfulness or
contentment in his ethical writings, defining the general
goal of life as joy, contentment or tranquillity, and locating
it in the soul. But it is above all for the theory of atomism
that both he and Leucippus are remembered.

From the 'seeds' of Anaxagoras, it was not an
impossibly large leap to the postulation of some kind of
elemental particle. However, the Atomists started off
from the one thing Anaxagoras refused to countenance:
an indivisibly small unit of matter.

'Atom' means, literally, 'uncuttable', that is, indivisible. Leucippus proposed that the universe consists of two basic constituents: indivisibly small atoms, of which an infinite number (but not an infinite variety) exist, and void or nothingness, which is also infinite, and in which the atoms move eternally. There is 'a limitless quantity of shapes among them (since there is no more reason for them to have one shape than another)'. From Democritus (via Aristotle) we learn that 'the substances are so small that they escape our senses', though they can differ in size, shape, order and position. The atoms move in the void, bouncing off each other or joining together in clusters: they are conceived as having tiny hooks and barbs on their surfaces by means of which they stick together temporarily before moving apart again and recombining with other atoms; in this way they form the objects of the sensible world. These objects are changeable, as the atoms cluster and dissociate, but the atoms themselves are not. The qualities of the clusters (hardness or softness, smoothness or roughness and so on) depend on the way the atoms have combined, for instance the tightness or looseness of the clusters. Sense perception could be explained by the action of atoms on the sense organs. For the Atomists, everything, even the soul, was made of atoms; Aristotle understood Democritus to say that thought itself is a physical process. Yet Democritus also argued that objects of perception and their qualities do not really exist; only atoms and the void exist.

Atomism constituted a systematic, internally coherent natural philosophy explaining everything in the perceptible world. What is innovative about the theory is that it never suggested that the movement of atoms is governed by any intelligence or intentionality, divine or otherwise, either operating upon or inherent in the primal substance. Atomism appears as the first truly materialist answer to Heraclitus' *Logos*, Parmenides' One, Empedocles' Love and Strife, and Anaxagoras' *Nous*. By positing indivisible units of matter, the atomists were also providing an answer to Zeno's paradoxes showing that motion is impossible.

Atomism was extremely influential. It was taken up by **Epicurus**, an Athenian philosopher of the generation after Aristotle, and thence adapted further by the Roman philosophical poet **Lucretius** (see chapter 11). Less directly, it seems to have had some influence on Plato, who in the *Timaeus*, his only dialogue to address physical theory extensively, presents a theory based on a different conception of indivisibles. We cannot trace a direct line from ancient atomism to the modern atomic theory of the twentieth century, for it was not a scientific theory resting on experimental method. Yet, lacking the advantages of experimentation, Leucippus and Democritus theorized a purely materialist explanation of the world, using concepts that prefigure, however distantly, the way we understand the structure of matter today.

❯❯ Key Ideas

- **Empedocles:** The universe is a closed sphere in which motion and change is constant; matter consists of four elements governed by Love and Strife.

- **Anaxagoras:** The universe is filled with an infinite number of seeds of matter, governed by *Nous*.

- **Atomism:** The two fundamental constituents of the natural world are indivisible units of matter, called atoms, and void or nothingness. Both the number of the atoms and the extent of the void are limitless. The atoms move about and combine and recombine in clusters, forming the substances and objects of our world. While these bodies consisting of clusters of atoms are subject to change and decay, the atoms are everlasting.

Chapter 7

Thinking for a Living – the Sophists

Discussion of the Sophists centres as much on method as on content. The word *sophistes*, apparently a word invented only in the fifth century BCE, means someone whose calling is that of wisdom or knowledge, and it came to be applied to peripatetic professional teachers, who travelled around teaching the rhetorical and language skills necessary to argue a case and other practical capabilities needed by men engaged in politics and the law, rather than theorizing about nature for its own sake. As itinerant teachers they did not found schools, but as participants in the dialogues of Plato, their posterity came to be assured. Very few of the sophists of whom we have record were born in Athens, but, if Plato is to be believed, they nearly all visited it, and the two key figures, Protagoras and Gorgias, settled there.

The sophists were highly influential in the development of the method of adversarial debate and advocacy, and in promoting a sceptical, questioning approach to knowledge and judgement. But they did not entirely abandon speculation about the nature of the world. In particular, they thought about knowledge and its relation with reality.

Sophism arose from specific social and political conditions in fifth-century Greece, and particularly

Athens. By 449 BCE the long and exhausting wars with Persia, which had dragged on for half a century, were definitively over, and a peace agreement was signed between Persia and Athens. Major victories over the Persians at Salamis in 480 and Plataea in 479 BCE had boosted the Greeks' confidence and engendered a certain sense of superiority over other cultures that was to persist throughout the Athenian 'golden age'. The last phase of the wars had seen the rapid rise of Athens: as leader of the Delian League, formed in 478/7 BCE to pursue the naval war against

Persia, it became the most powerful city-state in the Greek world. City-state government and in particular Athenian democracy had become consolidated.

In the 450s Pericles introduced political reforms that broadened the base of participation in the Athenian Assembly by introducing a stipend for those carrying out public duties, enabling poorer citizens to take part in government. This generated more debate as those who wished to wield influence in the Assembly, which took decisions by majority vote, needed to win over more voters. The profession of sophist grew up to meet this new need. Its practitioners' clients were mostly rich, aristocratic young men, and their fees were notoriously high, if we are to believe Socrates in Plato's dialogue *Hippias Major*: the democratization of education was never really a concern for either the sophists or their detractors. The political system may have become more democratic (according to its own limited criteria of citizenship and political participation), but the people who ran it were still upper-class men.

The social changes of the fifth century meant that philosophy turned its attention away from questions about the nature of the physical universe toward problems of the nature of knowledge, morality and justice. They brought in their train changes in ethical concepts and the questioning of old certainties: ideas of 'good' and 'justice' no longer meant what they had meant before – indeed they seemed to mean different things to different people – and new definitions were needed. Thinking about ethics began to raise its head.

On the whole, then, the sophists did not concern themselves greatly with cosmological or physical speculation (although some of them did make advances, for instance, in mathematics); they were more interested in studying how we know (and what is knowable) than in increasing the store of what we know. This concern had come to them from theorists such as Parmenides, and it was developed by both Protagoras and Gorgias, two of the principal sophists.

The sophists also claimed to teach 'virtue' – which they understood, for practical purposes, broadly as the

qualities necessary for a successful public career in a
city-state. This was the basis for the bad reputation
they acquired, principally from Plato, who mocked and
attacked them mercilessly in several works because they
'taught wisdom for money'. But Plato's idealism and
political conservatism were naturally antithetical to the
sophists' pragmatism and relativism. A central
preoccupation of much of his thought was to arrive at
impregnable definitions of goodness and justice. The
sophists, on the other hand, were more comfortable with
the shifts that were occurring in these concepts, and said
that such definitions depended on who was doing the
defining. They argued that some opinions are preferable
to others for particular people and particular purposes
(such as success in politics and public life), but they are
not necessarily more or less wise, or even truer.

This distrust of the idea of objective truth is in itself
a philosophical position, but one that entails some
difficulties. To the sophists, the real world was the
perceptible world, and it could be judged only on the
basis of subjective perception and experience and
empirical knowledge. Subjectivity was important
because, in their opinion, strict Eleatic concepts, and
even those of Anaxagoras, which held that sense
perception and common sense are unreliable, were
useless, even dangerous views to hold in practical life.
Yet there were other dangers involved in relativist
arguments. One such argument, which Plato relates in
the dialogue *Theaetetus*, is that a wind may seem cold
to one person and hot to another, meaning that things
acquire their specific nature only in the way they are
perceived, and that they have no objective nature

beyond our perceptions of them. This seems
uncontroversial when applied to simple things like
temperature, but the same process of reasoning is
riskier when transferred to moral judgments, such as
whether Hitler was a good man or not. Yet the sophists
were certainly not concerned to promote a moral
attitude of 'anything goes' in practice. For all his
opposition to him, Plato lets Protagoras say that

> ... wise and good orators make good things seem just
> to their cities instead of pernicious ones. Whatever in
> any city is regarded as just and admirable is just and
> admirable in that city for so long as it is thought to
> be so.

What Protagoras is defending here is not that there
is no such thing as justice, but that it means different
things in Athens and Sparta and Corinth; and it would
have been the job of the sophists to instruct young
leaders-to-be in any or all of the cities in how to be just
according to the rules and customs of their own city.
Far from advocating amorality, Protagoras seems to
have been advising his students to abide by the
conventional moral values of their own communities
and promoting a concept of collective self-interest as
the basis of practical justice.

PROTAGORAS

(c. 485–411 BCE):

Protagoras was the first and arguably the greatest of
the sophists, like Democritus a native of Abdera, and
the first sophist to come to Athens. He was a friend of

Pericles and suffered the fate of many friends of
Pericles, being accused of 'impiety' and having to leave
Athens in a hurry: he was apparently drowned in a
shipwreck on his way to Sicily.

We know of Protagoras' ideas chiefly through Plato,
which is unfortunate, since Plato usually sets these
ideas up only in order to demolish them. Protagoras has
become generally known as 'the father of relativism' – a
label that shows him to have been diametrically
opposed to everything Plato stood for. His chief claim to
fame is the familiar, and endlessly debated, aphorism,
'Man is the measure of all things'. In this he was
suggesting that there is no reality apart from what we
perceive. And if our perceptions are the guarantee of the
reality of things, then the centre of the universe is
humanity. However we interpret it, 'Man is the measure
of all things' makes it clear that Protagoras accepted no
absolutes existing anywhere beyond human perception
and judgment, as regards the nature of the gods, the
nature of the world around us, or the nature of 'virtue'
and 'justice'. Taken to their logical conclusion, these
ideas could legitimate the rejection of any kind of law or
morality. But as the case above suggests, Protagoras did
not seem to have adopted or promoted such attitudes.

He was also an agnostic: while not disbelieving in
the gods, he questioned the possibility that humans can
know about them. His treatise about the gods began:

*Concerning the gods, I have no means of knowing
whether they exist or not or what they might be like.
Many things prevent knowledge, including the
obscurity of the subject and the brevity of human life.*

These statements of Protagoras must not be taken to imply that he was not interested in truth. On the contrary, he was interested in the limits of knowledge and how truth itself could be judged. His key insight was that truth requires a measure external to itself, and he decided that the best available measure was human knowledge and experience, and that truths are not objectively true without reference to anything else but hold true within systems of thought or collectivities, such as the city.

In a work called in Latin *Antilogiae*, Protagoras laid out the ideas that Plato and others thought so pernicious, namely instructions on how to argue both sides of a question with equal success. As a logical exercise and a teaching aid, this might seem to many of us today to have been quite useful, but to Plato it was immoral and inimical to the attainment of true wisdom. Yet these ideas came to be seen as the defining characteristic of sophism. It is a pity that this emphasis has overshadowed Protagoras' more interesting ideas about the subjective nature and the limits of knowledge.

GORGIAS
(483–378 BCE)

The eloquent and long-lived Gorgias arrived in Athens as an ambassador from Sicily in his middle age, in 427, and spent most of rest of his life there, though he visited many other cities. An extreme sceptic, he wrote a treatise called *On Nature, or the non-existent*, in which he apparently refuted all possible views on existence and non-existence, claiming that nothing exists; or if it does, it is unknowable; or if it is knowable, we cannot articulate it to anyone else. He seems to have been influenced by Empedocles (also a Sicilian) and Zeno.

Once Protagoras had reduced reality to subjectively perceived experience, it was not difficult for Gorgias to make the transition to complete scepticism. In the area in which he was most influential, that of rhetoric, a relativistic approach lent itself readily to the art of using words to make things appear true and just to others irrespective of their objective truth (which he argued was unknowable). He was especially interested in the effects of speech and language on the emotions, and mentions the way tragedy can inspire pity and fear, thus prefiguring Aristotle's views on the effect of tragic drama in his *Poetics*. In a defence of Helen of Troy, who was traditionally held responsible for the Trojan War, Gorgias even went so far as to claim that words are by their very nature deceptive and fraudulent and that Helen was innocent because she had been overcome by the power of persuasion:

> *For speech constrained the soul, persuading it …*
> *both to believe the things said and to approve*
> *the things done.*
> (*Encomium of Helen*, trans. George Kennedy)

At the same time he was himself a stylistic innovator, applying to prose the figures of speech and rhetorical effects usually confined at the time to poetry. Plato criticized him in the dialogue that bears his name, arguing for the distinction between rhetoric and philosophy.

Other Sophists

We know of a number of other sophists, at least partly because Plato includes them as characters in his dialogues. **Prodicus** came up with a utilitarian explanation of traditional theology, suggesting that the sun, moon and other heavenly bodies were regarded as divinities because they were useful to the development of human society. The polymathic **Hippias** appears in two dialogues of Plato named after him, being ironically criticized by Socrates for getting rich from teaching. He is interesting for having made, possibly for the first time, the distinction between law (*nomos*) and nature (*physis*) as the basis for morality. This view was developed further by **Antiphon**, who asserted more radically that nature is 'truth' and its edicts 'compulsory', whereas human law is mere 'opinion' arrived at by 'consent', and that it is preferable to break human law in order to follow natural law than the reverse.

Thrasymachus is represented in Plato's *Republic* as putting forward the thesis that justice can be defined as the interest of the stronger and that governments make laws for their own advantage. This is the kind of argument that earned the sophists a bad name; but there is a strong philosophical point in Bertrand Russell's approval of them because they 'were prepared to follow an argument wherever it might lead them', even though that place was often one of profound scepticism. Russell says, 'The pursuit of truth,

when it is wholehearted, must ignore moral
considerations; we cannot know in advance that
the truth will turn out to be what is thought
edifying in a given society.'

» Key Ideas

- The social changes occurring in fifth-century Greece, and in
  particular Athens, resulted in a shift in the focus of philosophy
  away from the physical nature of the universe to human
  questions of knowledge and morality.

- Sophism was a profession, not a philosophical school. It answered
  new political needs, in particular the need to debate and argue
  persuasively in public life. Rather than exercising their minds on
  pure theory, the sophists made a living preparing aristocratic
  youths for public life, teaching rhetoric and the use of logic to win
  arguments. They could be seen as the first life coaches.

- The sophists were relativists: they held that there were no
  absolutes and that human experience and perception were the
  only real measures of truth. They asserted that moral values
  could vary with circumstances and in particular from city to city.
  However, they did not imply that relative moral values meant
  no moral values.

Chapter 8

Socrates

*Everything must be doubted, all presuppositions
given up, to reach the truth.*
(Hegel on Socrates)

We possess not a word written by Socrates. It is most
likely that he never wrote anything down: that would
have been unusual for a fifth-century Greek intellectual,
but then Socrates was atypical in many ways. It is
also very doubtful that he ever headed a school or
propounded a specific doctrine. But we know a great
deal about him from his best-known student, Plato,
nearly all of whose works are written in the form
of dialogues or debates between Socrates and his
students or other people. In the dialogues Plato brings
Socrates vividly to life: we know more about his
appearance, his personal circumstances and his way
of life than about those of practically anyone else in
Greek history. It is overwhelmingly through Plato that
Socrates' highly influential ideas have entered the
history of philosophy.

Plato was not the only student of Socrates to write
dialogues based on conversations with him, but he is
the most famous. The Athenian writer **Xenophon**, best
known as a historian, was also a student and friend of
Socrates, and wrote several works featuring him – a

Defence of Socrates, a four-volume *Memoirs of Socrates*, and a couple of short pieces of discussion with Socrates as a character, including, bizarrely, one on estate management. But his influence as a philosopher was much less than that of Plato, one of the most influential thinkers of all time, so it is Plato's image of Socrates that has become the standard. The comic dramatist **Aristophanes**, a closer contemporary of Socrates, painted a far less sympathetic picture of him in *The Clouds*, portraying him as a stereotypical sophist; Socrates apparently brushed the lampoon off with the remark that if it was deserved it would do him good, and if not, no matter.

Who was Socrates?

Thanks chiefly to Plato, we can put together a detailed biography of Socrates. Born about 468 BCE, he was the son of a sculptor or stonemason and a midwife (he must be one of the very few people in antiquity whose mother's job we know of – but, as we shall see, there is a reason for this). He served in the Athenian army as a hoplite, or heavy-armed infantryman, which suggests that he was comfortably off at the time, since he would have had to provide all his own armour and weapons;

but he fell into poverty in his later years, probably because he refused to take payment for teaching. Late in life he married a woman named Xanthippe. He participated in politics and managed to get on the wrong side of two governments. On the first occasion, in 406 BCE, during the Peloponnesian War, he went against the will of the Assembly in refusing to condemn the generals under whose command the crews of twenty-five Athenian warships had been lost in a storm at sea while returning from the battle of Arginusae, arguing that the condemnation was illegal under normal Athenian law. The second time, he was tainted by his association with the 'Thirty Tyrants', the oligarchic government imposed on the defeated Athens by victorious Sparta at the end of the war in 404 BCE. Two of his students, Critias and Charmides, had been among the Thirty. This second error proved fatal: Socrates was arrested when democracy was restored in 399, tried and executed by a lethal dose of hemlock.

Plato even tells us what Socrates looked like: he was far from handsome, but had great stamina and indifference to personal comfort. We learn from Plato also that Socrates was morally and physically courageous and had a highly developed sense of duty. He was kindly, generous and humorous; the Socrates of the dialogues certainly deploys plenty of wit, though it is sometimes waspish.

As for his work as a philosopher, it seems to have been carried out entirely in the form of conversations held in various houses and other places around the city; that, at least, is the impression we get from Plato and, to a lesser extent, Xenophon. Socrates did not write treatises; he did not promulgate doctrine; he did not produce universal theories about the world; as far as we can see he talked to individuals and small groups of people on topics that were, or should have been, close to their hearts and within their experience: ethical issues such as goodness, justice, courage, knowledge and love.

The Death of Socrates

It might seem odd to devote specific attention to someone's death, but that of Socrates was not only well documented but reported on by Plato in a way that illuminates various aspects of his thought. Socrates' trial and death are recorded in four works by Plato: *Euthyphro*, in which Socrates, on the way to his trial, meets a man who is prosecuting his own father on a matter concerned with religious piety; the *Apology* or *Defence of Socrates*, an account of his trial and his speech to the Assembly in his own defence; *Crito*, in which Socrates' friends visit in him prison two days before his death and try unsuccessfully to persuade him to escape; and *Phaedo*, a moving treatment of the last day of Socrates' life and his death. In each of these Plato takes the opportunity for a discussion of a relevant theme. In *Euthyphro*, Socrates deconstructs some accepted notions of piety and holiness and their relation to justice. In the *Apology*, as well as refuting the various charges against him, he tells how he came to the conclusion that he was not wise and developed his method of cross-questioning in an attempt to find wise men and increase his own wisdom. In *Crito*, the suggestion that his friends might get him out of prison provokes a discussion on whether or not it is right to break the laws of the state even if a conviction is unjust; and finally, in the later *Phaedo*, there is an important discussion of the soul, its immortality and what might happen after death.

Socrates is the first (though not the last) philosopher we know of to have been executed by a government. He was executed not for his beliefs, however, but because he was on the wrong side politically. It seems fairly clear that the charges against him, 'impiety' or 'introducing new divinities' and 'corrupting the young', were trumped up, since an amnesty had been granted to the opponents of the restored democracy protecting them from direct vengeance. Corruption of the young did not, incidentally, refer to any homosexual offence: in ancient Greece,

erotic relations between men, and especially between an adult man and a boy in his late teens, were not only not generally frowned upon but widely regarded as a beneficial mentoring process.

Socrates was religious and several times during his life, including during his trial, said he had received divine signs or warnings from a being he described as his *daimonion*, the 'little spirit' that guided his actions. His dying remark was 'Don't forget to sacrifice a cockerel to Asclepius' (the god of healing). The English philosopher Simon Critchley takes this rather

⊙ The Death of Socrates (*detail*), by Jacques-Louis David, 1787

inconsequential-seeming parting shot to have a deeper meaning, that Socrates wants to thank the god for relieving his ailment: death itself is the cure for life.

The Socratic Method

Much of Socrates' fame during his lifetime, and ever since, has rested on the way he carried out philosophical enquiry. Although he strongly disapproved of the sophists, almost certainly his method owes something to theirs, and in particular to their fundamental aim – to persuade and teach, rather than to theorize. This method was known in Greek as *elenchus*, cross-examination; in English, it is called 'dialectic', the process of arriving at a truth by means of question and answer. This is a method that cannot be carried out alone. We do hear of Socrates meditating or spending hours lost in thought, but he never pontificated: he elicited information from others and, by testing it and exposing its contradictions, enabled them to make their own discoveries.

Socrates was disingenuous about his own abilities. On the one hand he had been declared the wisest man in Greece by the Delphic oracle; on the other, he himself frequently said he knew nothing, and that the Delphic oracle called him the wisest man in Greece precisely because he had admitted to knowing nothing. He is drawing a distinction here between knowledge and wisdom, while also declaring himself to be open-minded enough to receive – even to draw out – the opinions of others, listen to them, and examine them.

This process of drawing-out Socrates described as midwifery. The metaphor refers to his mother's actual profession, but what Socrates brings to birth are ideas. In Plato's *Theaetetus*, Socrates says that rather than having ideas of his own, he 'delivers' other people's ideas. Though he himself is not particularly wise, people who associate with him who may at first seem 'pretty stupid' make 'astonishing progress' by discovering things within their own consciousness and 'giving birth' to them with Socrates' help. On the other hand, the *elenchus* sometimes ends by reducing to complete bewilderment an interlocutor who began by thinking he knew what he was talking about. Socrates loved to use relentless questioning to cut away familiar ground from under his interlocutors' feet and force them to abandon accepted ideas and attitudes. In this he often seems more like a terrier than a midwife.

The questioning method also means that Socrates didn't have to be consistent, but could put forward a variety of possibilities for consideration. For instance, the discussion of death in *Phaedo*, in which he argues for the immortality of the soul, is different from his approach in the earlier *Apology*, where he offers two alternatives: either death is just the end, the cessation of consciousness, or the soul goes somewhere else – perhaps a reminiscence of the Pythagorean belief in the transmigration of souls.

Socrates' Philosophy

As soon as we begin to discuss Socrates, we see that the ground of philosophical enquiry has shifted radically. In his early years he had been interested in natural philosophy, but by the time he becomes well

known to us, possibly before the outbreak of the
Peloponnesian War in 431, he had turned his attention
wholly to moral issues. With Socrates, human beings
and their actions and motivations take centre stage,
and philosophy starts in earnest to address good
and evil, right and wrong, justice and injustice, love
and beauty.

Socrates' way of doing philosophy was informal,
and different ideas on his key themes appear at
different stages in Plato's dialogues, but his thought
was not a disorganized ragbag of opinions; there are
identifiably coherent themes and lines of reasoning.
According to Aristotle, the two main contributions to
philosophy that could be attributed to Socrates were
the establishment of general definitions and the use
of inductive arguments – arguments that use particular
examples to arrive at a general point or principle.

Socrates has been called the first thinker to
emphasize the importance of arriving logically at
systematic general definitions of the moral terms to be
used in discussion, such as virtue, knowledge, justice
and so on. This involved questioning commonly held
assumptions about these moral categories. For
Socrates, the source of moral integrity as a universal
value could not be found in the traditions, customs and
practices of any one community. Where the sophists
had looked at definitions of justice and other moral
categories as applied to the societies of different city-
states, Socrates searched for universal concepts of
them that would hold good anywhere and for anyone.

Trying to establish these universal principles from
particular cases is a very common feature of Socrates'

method, although very often this kind of argument ends up disproving rather than proving the point and necessitating further debate. In Plato's dialogue *Meno*, for example, Socrates asks for a definition of virtue. Meno replies with various particular cases illustrating the traditional Greek concept of virtue as the fulfilment of social function: for a man it is skill in managing affairs of state, 'helping friends and harming foes'; for a woman it is running the household; and so on. Socrates wants something more general; Meno picks out a common feature in his previous definitions and says, 'It is to govern and rule over others'. Socrates objects that this can't apply to children or slaves. In the end the question remains unanswered, the only result being that Meno has successively abandoned all his positions. The example seems to have been introduced precisely in order for Socrates to define what virtue is *not*.

Definitions arrived at by this method seem often to be negative. Particular cases constantly turn out to disprove the general principle: for instance, someone suggests a definition of justice as paying one's debts; but there always turn out to be exceptions to the rules – is it just, for example, to pay taxes to a government which then uses your money to oppress its citizens? – and Socrates doesn't provide the answer. The only conclusion is that there are no watertight, universally applicable definitions of moral virtues. In fact, in Plato's *Protagoras*, Socrates ends up in a position of scepticism about the possibility that virtue can be taught at all (though Plato takes a different position later on, in the *Republic*, which may reflect his own opinion rather than Socrates').

However, complete moral relativism is not the answer either. A recurring, and much debated, Socratic theme is knowledge and its relationship to virtue, complicated by the idea that an overarching, general concept of virtue must embrace other, particular virtues – justice, courage, piety, and the rest – all of which also depend on knowledge. Since Socrates does not manage to prove identity between knowledge and virtue by argument, there may be a clue in the connection he draws between knowledge and self-knowledge, hinted at in the admonition 'Know thyself' that was inscribed on the temple at Delphi. 'Knowing what we are, we shall know how to take care of ourselves, and if we are ignorant we shall not know', says Socrates in Plato's first, disputed dialogue named for Alcibiades. This brings us a step closer to establishing knowledge's connection with virtue. Virtue then must involve something beyond just doing good or being good at things, something in the soul involving self-knowledge, or what has been called the subjective morality of individual conscience; something that it may be impossible to define by inductive argument.

» Key Ideas

- Socrates marks a new focus in philosophy on human agency and moral values – ethics takes centre stage.

- The method he used to discuss these ideas was dialectic, the art of using question and answer in dialogue to arrive at a truth. While the technique itself owed something to the rhetorical methods of the sophists, it was put to a very different purpose – the investigation of moral values at a general level.

- A central concern of Socrates was to establish general, universal definitions of moral values such as virtue, justice, courage and the like, drawing them out from particular cases by questioning. This was not easy, and often the argument from particular cases served only to unseat the proposed universal definition.

- Socrates distinguished between knowledge and wisdom. He saw the aim of philosophy as the improvement of the soul rather than the accumulation of factual knowledge, and he wanted his interlocutors to think for themselves rather than uncritically accept traditional or customary views.

Chapter 9

Plato

Imagine a group of prisoners sitting in a cave, shackled in such a position that they can look in only one direction, towards the cave's back wall. They cannot even look at each other. A fire behind them casts the shadows of objects on the wall. They have been there since early childhood, so they know nothing else. In the absence of any other experience, they accept the shadows as reality.

Now imagine that they are suddenly set free. As they turn and face the cave entrance, they are dazzled by light and at first cannot see anything clearly. They need to accustom themselves gradually to the light by looking at lesser lights such as the night sky or reflections in water, then progressing to ordinary daylight, slowly coming to know what 'real' reality is. Finally they can look at the sun itself and realize that it is the source of the daylight that illuminates the reality all around us.

This is Plato's most famous image, and he uses it to explain his most famous idea: that the world as we perceive it through the senses (the cave) is only a shadow of true reality, whose blazing light is the world of Ideas or Forms (the sun) perceptible only to the intellect or the soul (which escapes from the cave). We shall discuss this idea in more detail below; it is introduced here to give a taste of the dramatic imagination which, combined with meticulous reasoning, makes Plato such an approachable and rewarding philosopher today, even when we don't agree with him.

Plato's Life

Plato was born in Athens in 427 BCE into old money; he was descended from Solon, one of the Seven Sages (see chapter 2), he said. Various members of his family put in appearances in the dialogues, notably Critias and Charmides, relatives of his mother, who were among the Thirty Tyrants (see chapter 8). He possibly started out as a playwright, which might partly account for his decision to express his philosophy in a dramatic, semi-fictionalized form, even if it doesn't account for his notorious hostility to theatre. He was one of Socrates' most devoted and brilliant students. Disillusioned by the civil conflict preceding his mentor's death, he refused to enter politics when Socrates was executed and for a while withdrew to Megara on the Corinthian isthmus with some other disciples of Socrates. Involvement in politics seemed inescapable, however, and on a visit to Sicily in 387 he began a long friendship with Dion, a

Syracusan aristocrat, which caused him considerable
trouble over the next thirty years, not least because
Dion tried to foist on the city a government deliberately
formed along Platonic lines.

Soon after this trip, he began to teach near a grove
dedicated to the hero Academus on the
outskirts of Athens. This became the
Academy, Europe's first university. It lasted
as an institution till 529 CE, when the Roman
emperor Justinian dismantled it. It was not
just a think tank: it shared with the
Sophists the aim of educating young
men for public life, though it differed
from them radically in style and focus,
and included philosophy, mathematics
and astronomy in its curriculum. Plato
taught there for the rest of his life,
interrupted only by two further visits to
Syracuse, both traumatic. He died in 347,
handing the Academy on to his nephew Speusippus.

Both as a student of Socrates and chief transmitter of
his ideas to posterity, and on his own account, Plato has
had an immense influence on later thinkers. But, as a
result, there are different, often opposing, views about
almost everything he wrote. Some commentators
thought him a sceptic in the Socratic mould, others the
reverse, that he was dogmatic, advancing his own ideas
as doctrine. The Academy veered between these
positions in the generations after his death. Some praise
his idealism, others regard him as constrained both by
idealism and political conservatism, which would have
come naturally with his aristocratic social position and

connections but would also have been strengthened by his association with Socrates (a conservative but – unusually for a Greek philosopher – not an aristocrat). Like Socrates himself, Plato preferred to let people think things out for themselves rather than to tell them what to think, so he sometimes seems inconsistent.

Works

Plato is one of the few ancient philosophers whose published works have come down to us almost completely: nearly thirty dialogues, the *Apology* or *Defence of Socrates*, some letters, of which only the seventh is regarded as authentic, and some pieces of questionable authenticity. We don't really know in what order the works were written, and later Platonists made several different attempts to classify them. They can be roughly divided into three chronological periods: early, including the *Apology*, *Crito* and *Euthyphro*, which we met in chapter 8; middle, including three seminal works, *Phaedo*, *Symposium* and *Republic* (Plato's most frequently read work); and late, including *Parmenides*, *Statesman*, *Timaeus* and *Laws* (the last work). Overleaf is a list (in alphabetical order) of the works generally agreed today to be genuinely Plato's.

The dialogues cover a huge variety of subjects: knowledge, love, government, the arts, the nature of the soul, moral values such as justice, courage and pleasure, the purpose of life and the nature of being and reality itself. Only one work, *Timaeus*, is devoted to a theory of natural science; overwhelmingly, Plato's great themes are ethical and epistemological.

» Plato's Principal Works

- *Alcibiades*
- *Apology, or Defence of Socrates*
- *Charmides*
- *Clitophon*
- *Cratylus*
- *Critias* (unfinished)
- *Crito*
- *Euthydemus*

- *Euthyphro*
- *Gorgias*
- *Greater Hippias*
- *Hipparchus*
- *Ion*
- *Laches*
- *Laws*
- *Lesser Hippias*
- *Lysis*
- *Menexenus*
- *Meno*

- *Parmenides*
- *Phaedo*
- *Phaedrus*
- *Philebus*
- *Protagoras*
- *Republic*
- *Sophist*
- *Statesman*
- *Symposium*
- *Theaetetus*
- *Timaeus*

The Dialogue Form

Platonic dialogues are little dramas: vivid and colourful, they make Plato the most accessible Greek philosopher to a modern audience. But he didn't write them like this just to entertain. He deeply distrusted entertainment, and especially the power of dramatic representation to persuade people and influence their behaviour, usually not for the better. In his ideal society imaginative literature was either severely curtailed or outlawed altogether. He insisted on the distinction between language that seeks to persuade through its emotional appeal and the language of calm, rational argument.

So why did he choose this dramatic form – and a consciously crafted prose style – to express his ideas?

Since his quarrel with the arts was that they could so easily be used irresponsibly, he may well have been aiming to harness the obvious power of imagination to what he considered the most serious purpose conceivable: philosophical enlightenment.

An important effect of the dialogue, despite its attractive power as literature, is to establish distance between Plato and the reader. He uses this technique to make his readers think for themselves, just as Socrates did to his interlocutors. Rather than presenting his own conclusion, he takes his readers painstakingly through the steps leading up to it, until they can finally exclaim, with the interlocutors, 'Aha!' Of course Plato wants us to agree with his conclusions – and in the later, more 'dogmatic' works we are given less space to disagree – but he never forces us to agree with them uncritically, on his authority alone.

Plato, Socrates and Others

Socrates is by far the major influence on Plato's thought and its whole orientation towards ethical questions. He appears in all dialogues but the last (the *Laws*); Plato himself never appears. But Plato was hardly a mere scribe. The problem of where Socrates ends and Plato begins, of how to 'filter out' from the dialogues what could be ascribed purely to Socrates, leaving behind a coherent set of doctrines that could confidently be attributed to Plato, has long exercised scholars. The features of Socrates' thought discussed in the previous chapter are some of those that scholars attribute to

Socrates; but everything Plato reports of Socrates is inevitably overlaid with a Platonic patina.

Several Presocratic philosophers, many of whom were Socrates' contemporaries, have key roles in the dialogues and have dialogues named after them (*Protagoras*, *Gorgias*, *Parmenides*). Presocratic ideas underlie many of Plato's ideas: the Pythagoreans, Parmenides, Heraclitus and Xenophanes are some key influences besides Socrates.

Plato's Thought

In understanding Plato we face two problems: first, his ideas changed over time; second, they are never gathered together into boxes called 'Ethics', 'Politics', 'Cosmology' or the like, but are interwoven in different ways throughout the dialogues. We can notice a development, however, from the questioning of traditional virtues in the early dialogues to considering the wider implications of morality in social and political life, and finally to abstract reflection on logical, epistemological and cosmological issues. The early, 'Socratic' dialogues give no hint that the concepts of virtue and goodness being unpicked transcend human experience. By the middle period, and especially in the *Republic*, Plato is formulating a political order that embodies his moral ideals; but in this period we also meet the concept of Forms, which explicitly contrasts ordinary human life with experience of a transcendent ideal. Later still, Plato strove to link human experience with the order and purpose of the universe in a way that recalls Presocratic preoccupations.

Happiness and virtue

Plato saw the aim of human life as the attainment of happiness or well-being (*eudaimonia*) through moral virtue. In this he was not alone; but his concepts of *eudaimonia* and virtue are shifting and elusive. Over time, his ideas about virtue became increasingly austere and unworldly, finally uncoupling the pleasures of the soul from those of the body and declaring the latter inferior. As for happiness, he linked it ultimately with metaphysical concepts that seem at times almost impossible for ordinary mortals to understand or achieve. One wonders what his young students, prospective political and military leaders, thought of it all.

The early dialogues examine different kinds of virtue and seek definitions of them. We have glanced at some of these in the previous chapter. They work by exposing inconsistencies in order to point out that definitions of particular virtues in isolation are inadequate. In the *Protagoras* he (or rather Socrates) wants to reduce them all to knowledge. But, as we have seen, this definition is also found to be porous. Apart from anything else, it takes no account of the emotions or desires. It is not until the *Republic* that he unites the virtues in a hierarchy founded on wisdom rather than knowledge.

Love, sex and the family

Being a product of his society, Plato considered love between men superior to love between a man and a woman. But he didn't ignore women completely, and some modern feminists have even seen him as a proto-feminist. He abolished the family from his *Republic*, regarding it as a brake on the development of larger community structures and values. But where there was no family to be tended, what would women do? In the highly idealized *Republic*, Plato imagined women as warriors and philosophers, developing the same skills as men; in the less adventurous *Laws*, the family is allowed to exist to some extent. These proposals did not spring from any sense of essential equality between men and women, nor did Plato think further than allowing women to act like men; but he was the first philosopher to take women – if not gender relations – into account.

The physical love Plato discusses chiefly in the *Symposium* and *Phaedrus* is always between men. He idealizes the relationship between an older 'lover' and a younger 'beloved', stressing the elements of it that sublimate physical attraction into a relationship of intellectual and psychological care. His chief interest was in the relationship between such bonds in daily experience and the love of, and practice of, philosophy – not always an easy relationship, as he makes clear in the *Phaedrus*. In the *Symposium*, Socrates suggests that sexual desire can be transformed into the intellectual desire to know universal truths. This is called the ascent of love. People naturally desire what is good and beautiful; the ascent of love is the process by which they can learn to desire first bodily beauty, then the beauty of the mind, and finally the ideal or Form of beauty itself. The modern usage of 'Platonic relationship' to mean merely 'non-physical or non-sexual relationship', is a pale reflection of the idealist and transcendent concept of love Plato was trying to explain and advocate.

Government and society

Three works are specifically concerned with government and public life: the middle-period *Republic*, then the *Statesman*, and finally the *Laws*.

It is impossible to summarize the *Republic* briefly. It is a big, wide-ranging work in ten books, in which justice and injustice in the city and the individual soul are discussed at length, in parallel. Plato compares his model of the city, which has three classes of people (ordinary citizens, who produce for the city, soldiers, who protect it, and rulers, who govern it), with his model of the soul, which also has three parts (the appetitive, or the base and material desires, the spirited, the seat of courage and motivation, and the rational, which alone is capable of true intellectual activity). The rulers, the 'philosopher-kings', must be absolutely dedicated to the city's well-being, abjuring all personal aims; to do this they are prescribed an austere communal lifestyle without private property; their education, described in detail, takes about twenty-five years, and it is not till the age of fifty that they qualify to spend the rest of their lives alternately in governance and philosophical contemplation. The worker-citizens, by contrast, lead a much more comfortable material life but are considered of no intellectual worth; that is not their function, and virtue has been defined as the proper exercise of each citizen's appropriate function, without 'meddling in anything else'.

On the whole, Plato advocated keeping members of each tier in the hierarchy permanently at the level they were born into – 'lead', 'silver' or 'gold'. To maintain this in practice, he proposed that everyone should be taught that they were 'destined' by nature for their societal roles. Surprisingly he admits that this is in fact a 'noble lie' that must be taught to keep order and stability. Many later rulers have employed such a myth in their societies (often as a tenet of an established religion) to keep everyone in their place.

The *Statesman* asserts that government requires specialized expertise. A statesman must have both this expertise, which he is enabled to exercise entirely without hindrance or accountability to anyone, and dedication to the well-being of the city. The best form of government is rule by the expert; Socrates ranks other types of government in descending order of desirability, with law-abiding monarchy (distinguished from tyranny) at the top and democracy close to the bottom.

Socrates is absent from the *Laws*, which seeks to design the best legal system for a new city-state. Plato is somewhat more forgiving in his concept of the city here: he proposes a limited number of citizens (around 5,000), an assembly, a council and many public officers. Unlike both the *Republic* and the *Statesman*, this work sets a high value on law, and proposes a large number of laws that are set out in great detail. The role of philosophy is much weaker here, too, and is replaced by a rather repressive model of state religion.

The *Republic* is widely regarded as Plato's masterpiece, but there is no denying that its idealization of a rigidly class-based, totalitarian state headed by a philosopher-king who was supposed to embody virtue (but in practice could hardly be guaranteed to do so) is repellent to most modern readers. Plato was not a democrat – remember that the restored Athenian democracy had killed his beloved Socrates – and his model for the ideal state was closer to Sparta (historically conservative, oligarchical, setting great store by discipline, order and austerity) than Athens. His experiences of trying to realize the ideal state in Syracuse must also have been disillusioning, so it is not surprising that in the *Laws* Plato settles for a rather more democratic form of state as the realistic alternative.

The Forms

And what is the wisdom only philosopher-monarchs can attain, the thing they alone can contemplate, after all those years of rigorous training and self-denial? This raises Plato's signature idea: the theory of Forms.

As we saw in chapter 8, Socrates sought general or universal definitions of ethical values. In his middle dialogues Plato pursued this concern further and began to speak of 'Forms' or 'Ideas' as a higher level of universal. At the logical level, these capture what is common to all possible examples of a particular thing and express this as an abstract universal: in geometry, for instance, when we talk of a square, we are referring to the quality of squareness common to all square objects – and, moreover, we are thinking of a perfect, abstract square, since no material example of squareness is actually perfectly square. At the metaphysical level, Plato suggests that the Forms exist not just as theoretical concepts but that, on the contrary, they partake of a reality more real than any of their material instances. Material objects – and indeed ethical values and abstract concepts we encounter in the world – are mere shadows in the cave, reflections or copies of the true Forms of these things. In the *Phaedo* they are described as 'divine, deathless, intelligible, uniform, indissoluble, always the same as [themselves]'. The hierarchy of Forms culminates in the Form of the Good, which illuminates the rest as the sun does the earth.

The concept of the Forms is closely entwined with Plato's concern with defining true knowledge: the Forms (and only the Forms) are what is perceived by *episteme* – a pure and abstract kind of knowledge. As there is a hierarchy of objects or modes of being, there is also a hierarchy of modes of grasping them in thought, at the apex of which is *episteme*. Earthly things can only be the subject of 'opinion' or belief (*doxa*), though there is an intermediate mode of thought that grasps mathematical concepts. Philosophy, or dialectic, is the only route to knowledge of the Forms.

Knowledge of the Forms is also a kind of recollection (*anamnesis*), Plato says. He argues in the *Phaedo* that the soul is immortal and has the same qualities attributed to the Forms in the quotation above. It comes from a state of complete and perfect knowledge and forgets almost everything at (re)birth, but carries within it memories of perfect knowledge. This idea is linked to Pythagorean reincarnation, but also to the Socratic *elenchus*, whereby Socrates 'delivers' from people ideas or insights that he argues were 'in' them all along but just needed drawing out.

The theory of Forms became immensely influential, but we cannot be certain that Plato held a consistent view of it throughout his life. He began to develop the concept of the Forms in his middle-period dialogues and kept on developing it right up to the late *Parmenides*, where he presents six objections to the Forms that in the end more or less demolish them. The Forms appear in at least a dozen dialogues, but the arguments are never gathered together into a single sustained exposition, except when they are about to be subjected to critique.

The Universe, and God the Craftsman

Several of the later dialogues, including the *Theaetetus*, *Tinaeus*, and *Sophist*, put ethical problems on the back burner and concentrate on epistemological and cosmological questions. In the *Tinaeus*, Plato proposed a universe composed of indivisibles, and envisaged the four basic elements – earth, air, fire and water – as matter made up of isosceles and scalene right-angled triangles. Because the same triangles can recombine into different regular solids, the elements can transform into one another. Plato conceived of the triangles as indivisibles, giving this theory a flavour of atomism. More disputed is the view that Plato also thought of indivisible units of time.

The late dialogues also increasingly see a unity between human experience and the order of the universe. The *Sophist* deals at some length with being and non-being. The *Timaeus* introduces the idea of the divine Craftsman, who creates our world using the eternal Forms as a model. The Craftsman is good and wants to make the world as good as possible. Plato describes the 'ordered world' as the offspring of a union between Necessity and Reason, Necessity being understood as the irrational force that constrains cosmic Reason. The formation of the universe was the result of Reason's subjugation of Necessity. This theology had already been suggested in the *Republic*'s insistence that the gods are responsible only for good – a notion much more radical in Plato's own day than it seems to us.

Two strands of Platonic philosophy developed after Plato: the first, carried on in the Academy in the years immediately following his death, enquiring or sceptical, continuing or rescuing the Socratic method and openness of debate; the other doctrinal or dogmatic, regarding the preservation and promotion of Plato's literal ideas as fundamental. The latter tradition is the one that came to be understood and studied as Platonism.

>> Key Ideas

- As the cave analogy illustrates, Plato argued that the world perceived by the senses is not real; true reality is the realm of the Forms, transcendent and timeless templates, perceptible only to the soul, of both material objects and abstract concepts such as virtue and justice.

- He held that different kinds of knowledge correspond to these worlds; knowledge of the Forms can be attained only by philosophical debate (dialectic), aided by a kind of memory of perfect knowledge that the reincarnated soul retains.

- Plato's political views were authoritarian: he advocated a rigidly class-based system headed by philosopher-monarchs, those who had been trained over many years to perceive the world of the Forms.

Chapter 10

Aristotle

Forty-five years younger than his teacher Plato, Aristotle took from his studies at the Academy some fundamental concerns and principles that he developed further: crucially, the idea that logic was the tool by which philosophers could make coherent sense of the universe, and a concern with the problems of existence and knowledge.

Yet Aristotle was not a Platonist. He was very different from Plato in many respects, including intellectual temperament. He rejected the Forms and came to his own conclusions about the nature and causes of reality and how we can know them. He could not agree that the world we perceive through the senses was non-existent. Bertrand Russell called Aristotle's thinking about reality 'Plato diluted by common sense'. The impression we get from reading him is of a practical, common-sense thinker, steering a middle course and avoiding extreme positions in any respect, and in this he often seems to us more modern, if less romantic, than Plato.

Aristotle's Life

Aristotle was born at Stagira in northern Greece in 384 BCE. His family had a longstanding connection with the royal court of Macedonia, but between the ages of eighteen and thirty-eight Aristotle studied at Plato's Academy in Athens. He left the school after Plato's death in 347 BCE, possibly for political reasons but also because by then his views had diverged significantly from Plato's. After travelling and engaging in scientific research of various kinds in Asia Minor, he was summoned back to Macedonia to tutor King Philip's son, the future Alexander the Great. Again in contrast to Plato, he thought kings should not necessarily be philosophers but should have philosophers to advise them – even though Alexander followed little if any of Aristotle's advice. When Alexander condemned Aristotle's nephew Callisthenes to death, Aristotle left for Athens and in 335 BCE set up his own school, the Lyceum, where he taught for the next thirteen years. Many of his forty-seven surviving works date from this period. In 323 BCE Alexander died, an uprising against Macedonian domination was put down and – in a familiar political process of revolt and retaliation – Aristotle, tarred with the Macedonian brush, was accused of impiety on no real evidence and left Athens for good, dying the following year at Chalcis on the island of Euboaea.

Works

Aristotle studied and wrote on a wider range of subjects than probably anyone before or since. He had a passion for facts, research and classification, and owned a large library. As well as the surviving works, he is known to have produced some popular dialogues in his youth, and he made large collections of historical and scientific data, now lost. Only about a fifth of his known output has survived, and much of what we do have is apparently lecture notes for students, many edited by others. Aristotle's prose style is therefore far less elegant than Plato's – in fact it is often abrupt, allusive and obscure, though he favoured a simple, direct style for much of his subject matter.

In the list opposite the titles are given in English, although the scholarly tradition until very recently usually used the Latin titles given them by medieval scholars. Works of disputed authorship and works nowadays generally agreed to be not by Aristotle have been omitted.

Aristotle's Thought

Aristotle's work is too vast and diverse to summarize in a short chapter. But we can identify some connecting threads through his thinking on subjects

» Aristotle's Principal Works

Logic (*Organon*)
- *Categories*
- *On Interpretation*
- *Prior Analytics*
- *Posterior Analytics*
- *Topics*
- *Sophistical Refutations*

Physics (the study of nature)
- *Physics*
- *On the Heavens*
- *On Generation and Corruption*
- *Meteorology*
- *On the Soul*
- *Parva Naturalia* ('Little Treatises on Nature'):
  - Sense and Sensibilia [on sense-perception and its objects]
  - On Memory
  - On Sleep
  - On Dreams
  - On Divination in Sleep
  - On the Length and Shortness of Life
  - On Youth, Old Age, Life and Death, and Respiration
- *Researches into Animals* (*Historia Animalium*)
- *On the Parts of Animals*
- *On the Movement of Animals*
- *On the Progression of Animals*
- *On the Generation of Animals*

Metaphysics
- *Metaphysics*

Ethics and politics
- *Nicomachean Ethics*
- *Eudemian Ethics*
- *Politics*
- *The Constitution of the Athenians*

Rhetoric and poetics
- *Rhetoric*
- *Poetics*

as diverse as zoology and ethics: his passion for systematization and classification; his concern with teleology – the explanation of phenomena with reference to their purpose – and causation; and the characteristic Aristotelian principle of moderation, not only as regards human behaviour but also in more theoretical fields.

The branches of knowledge

Aristotle classified the branches of knowledge into three, each with several subdivisions:

- **practical**, dealing with human behaviour, in private and public life (addressed e.g. in *Ethics*, *Politics*);
- **productive**, concerned with making things, either beautiful (the visual arts, literature, drama) or useful (crafts, trades) (addressed e.g. in *Rhetoric*, *Poetics*);
- **theoretical**, dealing with truth itself, including mathematics, logic and the natural sciences (*physike*), but also a category Aristotle called 'theology'. This included the study of changeless substances, which Aristotle, like many of his predecessors, believed were divine, and which he considered the object of study of what he called 'First Philosophy' (see below).

Can we call Aristotle a scientist? This is an ongoing debate among both scientists and philosophers. Over the centuries, views of the distance between Aristotle's work and that of, say, Descartes and Galileo, have fluctuated. The separation we make today between 'science' – exact, experimental, concentrating, in Aristotle's terminology, on material and efficient causes (see below) – and 'philosophy', which was speculative, abstract, more concerned with his final causes, did not really apply in ancient Greece. The Greek word *episteme*, often translated into English as 'science', is just as often translated as 'knowledge'. It is a fluid term: it is fairly clear that Plato and Aristotle, for instance, meant rather different things by *episteme* and the objects it contemplated. To clarify: in this chapter the word 'science' is used as well as 'natural philosophy' to refer to those branches of knowledge explored by Aristotle that later fell under the umbrella of 'science' – that is, those in which we see him engaging in empirical, observational and classificatory, if not strictly experimental, research.

It is important to note that, as well as being a great speculative theorist, Aristotle was also a great ultimate empiricist: he not only attended to scrupulous empirical investigation of the details of his observable world, but held as a fundamental tenet that everything that comes into our minds has first been perceived by our senses. So the senses are, for Aristotle, the source of all our knowledge.

Logic and knowledge

Although Aristotle himself conceived of logic as a general, theoretical branch of philosophy, later thinkers debated whether it was a branch of philosophy at all, or a methodological tool, or both. The second view, upheld by Aristotle's own followers, resulted in the collective name given to his logical works: *Organon*, meaning 'tool'.

The six works of the *Organon* are the earliest known study of formal logic. They establish the logical rules by which Aristotle wanted the other branches of knowledge to be organized systematically. Aristotle did not invent logic, but he did invent the discipline of formal logic, as well as its terminology. Common philosophical terms such as 'syllogism', 'particular', 'universal', 'premise', 'conclusion' and the like are translations of the terms Aristotle used and are still in use today.

Aristotle sought to rest each of the sciences, or bodies of knowledge, on a limited number of fundamental propositions, or **axioms**, posited as primary truths about the subject, from which other truths (theorems) could be derived by reasoning. Deductive logic, which aimed to show how to do this, is a major topic, especially of the *Prior Analytics*. Aristotle devised a formal system for translating sentences into general formulae by substituting letters for particular subjects and predicates of sentences. This standard pattern of deductive argument is called the **syllogism.**

❯❯ The Syllogism

A syllogism is a form of deductive argument consisting of two premises from which a conclusion follows, for example:
All cats are carnivores;
All tigers are cats; therefore
All tigers are carnivores.

Aristotle (see chapter 10) discovered that, by replacing the specific terms (e.g. 'cats', 'carnivores', etc.) by letters, syllogisms could be expressed as a general arguments, e.g.:
All B are A;
All C are B; therefore
All C are A.

Aristotle's great innovation was to discover that this kind of deductive argument, whatever the subject matter, could be expressed quasi-mathematically as a general argument leading to a universal conclusion. Ultimately, the problem with Aristotle's syllogistic reasoning was that its internal consistency didn't guarantee the objective truth of the conclusions; but, although he did not succeed in producing an unassailable logical system, it is the fact of the innovation – the idea that deductive arguments can be expressed formally – irrespective of the flaws in it, that broke new ground.

In the *Posterior Analytics* and elsewhere Aristotle deals with induction, a reverse kind of argument; he characterizes it as argument 'from the particular to the universal' – the general categories that could be inferred from particular examples. Although he never dissects induction in as much detail as deduction, it is very important in his theory of knowledge, which, he declared, must be both systematic and explanatory. In order to devise his axiom-based system founded on universal truths, Aristotle wanted to know how we know what is true, and how we know that the things we know are true. He believed you could not really know something unless you could *explain* it, or give its 'causes'. It was not enough to know from observation that cats have claws; you had to know that they have claws for a reason, and what that reason was – to capture prey, to defend themselves, and so on. We shall explore this interest in causation and purpose further in the next section.

Much of the *Posterior Analytics* is an attempt to construct an axiom-based system for the sciences, or fields of natural philosophy; but it is not itself so systematic. As Jonathan Barnes points out, it is not a book of science but a book about how a science ought to be constructed. And in other works Aristotle did not present the various sciences axiomatically but in a rather more questioning, investigative way, with frequent reference to the 'reputable opinions' of his predecessors (for example, in the *Meteorology*, to Anaxagoras' ideas about the aether or Democritus on comets). (This tendency, incidentally, is what makes him such an excellent source for the Presocratic philosophers.) Systematization was always his ideal, and perhaps an impossible one, but the surviving treatises (in fields of study where, we must remember, he was often a pioneer) convey much more strongly a sense of systematization-in-progress – not yet a complete system, but aiming for it.

Purpose and cause

For Aristotle, **teleology** offered the best explanation for observable phenomena in the natural world: the nature of everything could be expressed in terms of its *telos*, the goal or end towards which it strove. Everything had its own immanent or inherent *telos* and a natural tendency to realize it. Thus the *telos* of a kitten would be the cat, that of a seed the plant into which it grows; kitten and seed reach their fulfilment when they develop into cat and plant. This idea is linked with Aristotle's concepts of potentiality and actuality, according to which everything contains the potential to become its *telos*: that is, the kitten contains the potential to be actualized as a cat (and only a cat).

These are simple examples, but Aristotle applies the theory widely. Every action, for him, involves the release of some kind of potentiality tending towards a final cause or actuality. Human beings have a *telos*, too; he discusses this in the *Nicomachean Ethics* and *Metaphysics*. He seems to distinguish between teleology involving agency or intention, which applies to human activities, and teleology pertaining to non-human organisms, which is merely immanent. He argues in the *Physics* that since carnivores have sharp teeth in front and broad, flat teeth at the back of their mouths in order to tear and then chew their food, the possession of such teeth is *for the purpose* of the carnivore's survival – an idea that has seemed to many to foreshadow natural selection.

The idea of the *telos* is thus linked with Aristotle's concept of causation. He identifies four 'causes' (*aitia*) of things: we call these (though Aristotle does not) material, formal, efficient and final. In the following example, he is not using the word 'cause' exactly as we would, for he simply uses the word *aition* for each 'cause':

- the *material cause* of a statue is the material of which it is made (bronze, marble, etc.)
- the *formal cause* is the idea or plan in the mind of the sculptor, or the subject of the statue;
- the *efficient cause* is the sculptor himself;
- the *final cause*, which is also the *telos*, is the purpose or reason for which the statue was made (to please a patron or honour a god, to be beautiful, to provide income for the sculptor, etc.).

The four causes are clearly more applicable to artefacts than to natural organisms, and Aristotle himself never makes it quite clear what he means by *aition* – in fact he warns explicitly in the *Physics* that the word is being used ambiguously. In particular, 'final cause' could be replaced by 'reason' or 'explanation', since it answers the question 'What for?' Aristotle puts the greatest emphasis on the 'Why?' or 'What for?' question in seeking understanding of any phenomenon: he derides the Atomists for only going as far as seeking explanations in terms of the first three 'causes' and omitting the most important cause – the final cause. Modern science, of course, restricts its discussion of explanations of natural phenomena precisely to the first three types of 'cause'.

As with many of Aristotle's theories, this one is not absolutely systematic, and variations appear in different treatises. But it was an important part of his quest for universal principles, and we can see its lack of conclusiveness today as foreshadowing a modern, open-ended scientific approach.

Biological researches

One respect in which Aristotle looks straight back to the Presocratic thinkers is in his concentration on the study of nature. Though he wrote important books on logic, ethics, politics, and the arts, much of his work was in natural philosophy (called 'physics' – *physike* in Greek); about a quarter of all his extant work treats themes related to what we call biology. It seems there was no aspect of the physical world on which Aristotle had nothing to say.

Some philosophers don't regard Aristotle's biological researches as part of his philosophy, seeing them as a different kind of enquiry. But the methods, and some of the insights, of these researches spilled over into other fields; it was, for instance, his study of living creatures and his sense that the organization of the natural world was not coincidental or haphazard that led him to the idea of *telos* – the idea that creatures were as they were for a reason or purpose.

During his time abroad after 347 BCE Aristotle explored zoology and biology, collecting, observing, and dissecting specimens. This resulted in two large books, of which *Historia animalium* (Researches into Animals) survives. It describes the anatomy of mammals, birds, reptiles and especially fish and other sea creatures, their reproductive systems, food, habitat and behaviour. Aristotle used this empirical evidence to devise a hierarchy of life forms from 'inanimate' matter to god, through plants, insects, sea creatures, reptiles, birds, mammals and human beings. His classification scheme was a huge conceptual advance on previous ones, and provided the basis of taxonomy for most of the next two millennia – a testament to its strengths, but also a brake on more independent research, for Aristotle was taken as the unquestioned authority, even though he was not always right and sometimes accepted hearsay evidence uncritically. None the less, in collecting, observing and recording so extensively he broke new ground of immense value for the future development of the biological sciences almost up to our own day.

Ethics and politics

Aristotle wrote several works on ethics, of which the most familiar is the *Nicomachean Ethics* (named possibly from its dedication to his son Nichomachus). He classified ethics as a practical science, and the ten books of the *Ethics* travel through a list of virtues – courage, temperance, liberality, greatness of soul, good temper, even the virtue of being good company – as well as discussing justice, pleasure and evil. That Aristotle took a teleological view of ethics, however, is clear from the very beginning of the *Nicomachean Ethics* (1094a1):

> *Every art and every inquiry, and similarly every action and choice, is thought to aim at some good; and for this reason the good has rightly been declared to be that at which all things aim.*

Thus, the *telos* of a person is *eudaimonia* (happiness), achieved through goodness. Aristotle spends the whole first book of the *Nicomachean Ethics* defining the good, concluding that a good individual is one who carries out his or her function well. This is not such a new idea, but Aristotle links it with the idea of potentiality and suggests that goodness is actualized as *eudaimonia*. What makes human beings different from all other creatures, he says, is the faculty of reason, and our proper function is to exercise that faculty well; consequently, *eudaimonia* is defined as acting in accordance with reason. Moral evil is seen as a failure to actualize the *telos*.

Aristotle was less idealistic than Plato, however: his *eudaimonia* could be achieved through action as well as thought and was not incompatible with health or wealth – though he thought lesser mortals such as women, slaves and foreigners were by nature incapable of achieving it. Yet his final concept of the highest, most godlike form of happiness has a Platonic flavour, for he defines it as a life spent in philosophical contemplation, although he is more forgiving than Plato insofar as he does not restrict such contemplation to the chosen few philosopher-kings but sees it as the actualization of the human *telos* – something that could presumably be carried out by every man.

A central idea in Aristotle's ethics is the famous concept of the mean, which at its simplest means avoidance of extremes in pursuit of the good life. Virtues, according to Aristotle, are a point of moderation between two vices: for instance courage is the mean between cowardice, at the one extreme, and recklessness, at the other; temperance is the mean between self-indulgence and neglect of one's own (reasonable) needs. The idea of the mean, in fact, can be detected in most aspects of Aristotle's thought. In politics, for instance, he illustrated the mean by advocating rule by the middle class; he disapproved of empire but valued stability highly.

As well as the *Politics*, Aristotle wrote accounts of the constitutions of several states, of which only the one on Athens survives completely. Yet his political views are neither idealistic nor adventurous and seem to us today somewhat blinkered by elitism. He did not question the social stratification of the city-state and seems hardly to recognize its decline as a political entity, even though he was there when Athens fell to the kingdom of Macedonia. His ethical and political views remain rooted in the life of the *polis*; even *eudaimonia* as he conceived it was only imaginable among a leisured male elite such as had already nurtured most of the Presocratic philosophers.

First philosophy

Aristotle never heard the word 'metaphysics'. We know one of his principal works as the *Metaphysics*, but this is not the title he gave it. 'Metaphysics' was merely a classification label given it by a later editor, referring to the works that came 'after the works on physics', possibly in a course of study, since Aristotle says this subject should be studied by those who have already studied nature (the main subject of the *Physics*). However, this treatise became so important to later scholars that the name stuck to the subject area that it had been the first to cover.

The *Metaphysics* ranges over many topics, often revisiting and refining ideas raised elsewhere. Chiefly, it addresses the highly general and abstract area of knowledge Aristotle called 'beings *qua* being' – that is, the study of things as regards their existence, rather than any other property they have, and thus the nature of existence itself. He thought this the highest branch of knowledge, because it deals with universals, and called it 'the first philosophy' – the study of primary things – and thus part of theology, which studies things that are non-material, changeless and eternal.

Aristotle had defined universals as representing the common properties of any group of real objects. Universal terms (such as adjectives and the abstract nouns derived from them, for example, red / redness, or happy / happiness) apply to classes of thing, not individual things. His treatment of universals in the *Metaphysics* frequently harks back to the logical treatises, in the attempt to establish what 'being' and 'substance' are (he suggests that they are actually the same); and he goes even further in asking what makes something a substance – what is the first, universal principle lying beyond being itself?

He concluded that this first principle had to be something that was changeless, motionless and eternal. Both the evidence of the senses and his study of other philosophers told him that change and movement were characteristic of the material world and the heavens. Matter consisted of the four earthly elements, fire, air, earth and water, each of which had four primary powers or qualities – hotness, coldness, wetness and dryness. Generation and decay occurred in the 'sublunary' region between the moon and the earth. His astronomical schema was largely adapted from that of two of his contemporaries, **Eudoxus** and **Callippus**: the spherical earth was at the centre of a system of concentric, moving celestial spheres, composed of a fifth, heavenly element, *aether*, which carried the sun, planets and stars.

In the *Meteorology* he had addressed the question of causation on the cosmic scale, suggesting that the elements were the material causes of events in our world, while 'causality in the sense of the original principle of motion' was located in the heavens, attributable to the 'influence of the eternally moving bodies'. Ultimately everything in motion is moved by an unchanging, eternal, motionless being, which is usually referred to as 'the unmoved mover' or 'the prime mover'. Though divine, the unmoved mover was not a creator, but a cause and explanation. It was the uncaused cause, the being beyond being, its potentiality perfectly actualized and at rest, the summit of Aristotle's hierarchy of nature.

In an extraordinary passage in the Metaphysics (1072b4), he links this final cause with goodness and love. The final cause, he says, is not only the good for something, but also the good towards which action tends. In this sense, of the good being that towards all actions move, 'it produces motion by being loved, and it moves the other moving things'.

Thus the unchanging 'prime mover' starts everything moving and keeps it moving, not by 'doing' anything – which would imply change and motion on its own part – but simply by being so attractive or desirable that everything else is moved towards it, or is moved to action for its sake.

❯❯ Key Ideas

- Aristotle loved classification: three branches of knowledge, each with subsets; four levels of causality: material, formal, efficient and final causes. In biology, his classification of living creatures became the standard for many centuries.

- He invented formal logic, in particular the form of deductive argument using syllogisms in which particular subjects and predicates were represented as general categories by letters.

- He argued that the nature of everything in the world could be expressed in terms of its *telos*, the goal or end towards which it strove. He also identified this goal as the 'final cause' in his system of causation.

- His thinking about universals and his 'metaphysical' theories are in part a development of, in part a response to, Plato's theory of Forms. Seeking a first principle or final cause, he postulated the existence of a divine 'unmoved mover' responsible for change in the universe while itself remaining motionless and changeless.

- Aristotle did not agree with Plato that the world we perceive through the senses was non-existent, and he argued that sense-perception was a reliable way – indeed, the only reliable way – of understanding the world. He regarded everything that enters the mind as having been first perceived as an observable object by the senses.

- In ethics and politics he advocated moderation (observance of the 'mean') in all things.

Chapter 11

Cynics, Stoics and Epicureans

'Cynical', 'stoical', 'epicurean': these words are used today to refer to attitudes or mindsets. They derive, however, from three schools of philosophy, one an offshoot of Socratic ideas that interpreted them differently from the Platonic mainstream, the other two post-Platonic schools that were diametrically opposed to one another.

The Cynics

The Cynics were not an organized school but a loose, fairly diverse group with no fully elaborated, systematic philosophy such as those of Plato or Aristotle. Their name comes from **Diogenes the Cynic** (*c*. 400–*c*. 325 BCE). 'Cynic' means 'doglike', and Diogenes acquired this nickname either because he rejected all social conventions and deliberately lived in primitive conditions (in a barrel, according to some stories) or because of his biting, satirical wit. The actual founder of the group was probably the less picturesque **Antisthenes** (*c*. 455–*c*. 360 BCE), a pupil of Gorgias who later became a disciple of Socrates. The Cynics promoted, as the path to happiness and virtue, a very simple, independent life unencumbered by possessions and social ties. They (or at least Antisthenes) were strongly opposed to Plato's theory of Forms: Antisthenes reportedly remarked to Plato, 'I can see a horse, but I can't see horseness.' Wisdom for the Cynics was the ability to understand that the values most people upheld were worthless, in contrast to the Socratic notion of analysing those values to seek a universal value beyond and above them.

The third important figure among the Cynics was **Crates** (c. 365–c. 285 BCE). A native of Thebes, he renounced a large fortune to live a life of Cynic poverty in Athens. He is said to have known of Diogenes, and was the teacher of Zeno of Citium, the founder of Stoicism.

The Cynic movement faded in the first and second centuries BCE but was revived in the first century CE.

The Stoics

'Grin and bear it' is the cliché of stoicism today. But there was more to the Stoics than that. Their name comes from the Stoa, the colonnaded portico in Athens where the first group of Stoics gathered with their teacher, **Zeno of Citium** (c. 335–263 BCE). It was a well-organized, long-lived and well-documented school, and the names of many of its representatives have come down to us. **Chrysippus** (280–207 BCE), the third head of the school, was said to have written over seven hundred books; he developed a different logical system from that of Aristotle, which was considered more important than Aristotle's in the Hellenistic period.

The Stoic school rejected not only Plato's theory of Forms (Zeno wrote a *Republic* in answer to Plato, with its own utopian society including women and slaves as citizens) but all theories about the unreliability of the senses as a source of knowledge, and took the empiricist view that, on the contrary, sense-perception is the starting-point of all knowledge. However, they did not recognize sense-perception itself as the criterion of truth, as the Epicureans did, observing that the evidence of the senses is not always and equally reliable. They argued that what defines the truth of a perception is the 'assent' that the mind gives to a sense-perception. As in Plato, true knowledge is distinguished from opinion, but in respect of the process by which it obtained, not the object of knowledge itself. Ordinary people are often deceived and give assent wrongly, but the wise man or 'sage' never holds mere opinions and always assents correctly.

In their cosmology the Stoics looked back to Heraclitus, the identification of the fundamental substance as fire and the concept of *logos*. In Stoicism the *logos* was the dynamic rational principle in the world; there was also an understanding of *logos* as the human faculty of reason that developed as a person grew from childhood to adulthood. Reality could only be understood by reason.

The early Stoics defined virtue as living in harmony with nature, and taught that a full understanding of the physical world and its laws would prevent us from expecting or desiring what was not going to happen, thus preserving us from disappointment. Their training concentrated more on 'wanting what you get' than on 'trying to get what you want'. They constructed a scale of different degrees of accordance with nature, calling many things morally indifferent. They identified four cardinal virtues—'moral insight', courage, self-control and justice—which they saw as indissolubly connected, so that the good person would have to have them all. Their message was stern: progress towards virtue was very slow and one usually attained it only late in life, if at all. Later Stoics laid more emphasis on the idea of progress. In another legacy of the Cynics, the Stoics also favoured renouncing all passionate emotions such as pleasure, sorrow, desire or fear, and aiming for a state of apathy (*apathia*), seeing this as a positive virtue rather than—as we would see it today—an undesirable state calling for a physical or psychological remedy. Here we see the genesis of the modern sense of stoicism.

The later Stoics, in particular in Rome, concentrated almost entirely on ethical questions. From the third century onward the school declined; but Stoic ideas were popularized and became influential, being carried forward significantly in Rome by **Seneca** (*c.* 5 BCE–65 CE) and the second-century emperor **Marcus Aurelius** (121–180 CE), and influencing early Christian thinkers.

The Epicureans

The school founded by **Epicurus** (341–271/70 BCE) rivalled Stoicism in Athens. The modern sense of an 'epicure' as a decadent *bon viveur* comes chiefly from a scurrilous anecdote one of the Stoics told about Epicurus – that overindulgence caused him to vomit twice a day. (Later, this habit could be attributed not unfairly to the entire ruling class of imperial Rome.) Diogenes Laertius paints a kinder portrait, praising Epicurus for his prolixity (thirty-seven books on natural philosophy, practically none surviving) and his abstemiousness. In his natural philosophy Epicurus espoused a theory of atomism; aiming to free people from the fear of death and the gods, he held that at death the soul simply dissolves into its constituent atomic particles. His idea of happiness was freedom from all desires and anxieties, including ambition and material possessions. He taught that the gods lived in the vast interstices among infinite numbers of worlds and had no interest in human life.

Epicureans lived in small communities removed from political society, in which women and slaves participated on an equal footing and friendship was supremely valued. Epicurus himself had set up a community in Mytilene on Lesbos and another in Lampsacus before returning to Athens and establishing a school, situated halfway between the Academy and the Stoa, which he called the Garden. He was the first philosopher to admit women to a formal school.

Epicurus' ideas made their way to Rome and were reproduced remarkably faithfully by the poet **Lucretius** (?94–?55 BCE), who translated Epicurus' physical theory into Latin, practically without alteration, in a long, six-volume poem of considerable stylistic merit.

» Key Ideas

- **Cynicism:** Promoted a simple, independent life untrammelled by possessions and social ties.

- **Stoicism:** Defined virtue as living in harmony with nature, without passions but with courage, temperance and morality. Adapted the Heraclitean cosmology.

- **Epicureanism:** Lived in community; espoused atomism and saw it as a guarantee against fear of death and the terrors of the afterlife.

Chapter 12

What Happened Next

> *It is [the Greeks] who have taught us, not to
> think—that all human beings have always done—
> but to think about our thinking.*
>
> (W. H. Auden, 'The Greeks and Us', *Forewords and Afterwords*)

Hellenistic Philosophy and Science

Greek philosophy did not end with Aristotle and his
contemporaries. In the period known as 'Hellenistic',
between Aristotle's death and the establishment of
Neoplatonism by **Plotinus** in the third century CE,
many important thinkers were active in the Greek
world. There were significant developments in the
sciences, particularly in the third century BCE. The rise
of Alexandria in Egypt as a centre of research and
scholarship, and the building of its great library and
museum under royal patronage, were important
catalysts for these advances.

Hellenistic philosophy grew out of the two great
schools of the late fourth century: Plato's Academy
and Aristotle's Lyceum. However, its ethical focus
shifted in accordance with the changes in politics and
society resulting from the Macedonian conquest of
Greece and the creation of a vast empire under one
ruler, extending well beyond Greece. In such a

society, individuals had few, if any, channels for contributing to political life, and, as we have noticed with the Stoics and Epicureans, philosophical interest centred far less on constructing visions of an ideal state, or the kind of state that would enable its  citizens to achieve happiness, than on personal morality and how individuals' actions and character traits might enable them to live well and happily whatever the political society they were living in.

Stoicism and Epicureanism continued to be influential well into the Roman imperial period, elements of them percolating into early Christian theology. As Christianity burgeoned, however, the Hellenistic philosophical schools declined. **Augustine** (354–450 CE) carried Neoplatonism into Christian thought, where it became a major influence.

The Hellenistic period saw greater specialization in the disciplines of natural philosophy, sharpening the distinctions between philosophy, mathematics and medicine already forming in the classical period.

Several Hellenistic figures are very familiar to us. The *Elements* of **Euclid** (*c.* 326–265 BCE), which developed and systematized Pythagorean and Milesian mathematical theories, became the standard geometry textbook right up to the mid twentieth century. **Archimedes** (*c.* 287–212 BCE), famous for his cry of 'Eureka!' (I've got it!), among other things invented a hydraulic screw as a mechanism for lifting water and established the formula for determining the volume of a sphere. In astronomy, the cross-fertilization of Greek and Babylonian astronomy became increasingly important.

To a large extent, however, the achievements of Hellenistic science have not been as universally recognized as the ideas of the classical thinkers. Some modern scholars contend that the 'Hellenistic scientific revolution' disappeared from view for many centuries between the Roman period and the Renaissance, when knowledge of the Greek world was revived, studied and enthusiastically imitated. The logical theory of the Stoics, for example, which had overshadowed Aristotle's logic during the Hellenistic period, sank almost without trace.

The overwhelming influence of Aristotle contributed to this. He dominated thinking in all fields of philosophy for a very long time. His works had a chequered history in the centuries after his death but never completely disappeared, for in the late first century BCE Andronicus, leader of an Aristotelian school in Rhodes, had had many copies made of each work. Between the first and the sixth centuries CE, they were analysed and discussed by many scholarly commentators. They also made their way to the expanding Islamic world, where the Aristotelian tradition was long preserved, the *Prior Analytics* and some other logical treatises being translated into Arabic possibly as early as the sixth century CE. As Muslim power in Western Europe receded after 1085 (the beginning of the Christian 'reconquest' of Spain), almost all of Aristotle's works then extant were translated into Latin by Western European scholars in the twelfth and thirteenth centuries, ensuring their dissemination through medieval Europe.

The Philosophical Legacy of Greek Philosophy

The current popular interest in ancient societies and classical studies often focuses on what the ancient world taught us. Of course, the legacy handed down by the Greek thinkers to succeeding ages is incalculable: the English philosopher Bernard Williams (1929–2003) is right in saying, 'The legacy of Greece to Western philosophy is Western philosophy.' The Greeks have seeped into our culture, and their ideas can be traced in it right up to the present, passing through the Renaissance and the eighteenth-century Enlightenment, when the lively interest in Pythagoras, Plato and Aristotle among the great Scottish philosophers earned Edinburgh the nickname of 'Athens of the North'.

Here and there in this book we have noticed the continuing influence of particular Greek philosophers on later philosophers and scientists, but the legacy goes deeper than that. Perhaps even more than *what* we think, Greek philosophy has conditioned *the way* we think. We remarked in chapter 1 that active questioning and reasoned argument are defining characteristics of Greek philosophy. That spirit of critique – the insistence on making informed choices between standpoints on the basis of reason and deduction rather than the acceptance of dogma or tradition – is fundamentally Greek. It is there in the conceptual tennis match between Presocratic monists and pluralists, and most of all it is there in the Socratic *elenchus*. Aristotle, too, is present in the concept of scientific methodology we think is self-evident, that abstract theory must be supported by empirical evidence.

Apart from the brief flowering of Stoic logic, Aristotle's formal logic was practically unchallenged until the twentieth century, when the work of Gottlob Frege (1848–1925) and Bertrand Russell exposed its limitations. Opinions of the similarities between Aristotle and modern logic have fluctuated, but a significant recent position is that modern mathematical logic may be closer to Aristotle than was previously thought.

The Natural Sciences

We have clearly far outstripped the Greeks in our understanding of the physical universe and how it works, and in the technology with which we can explore it, but we owe many discoveries and theoretical approaches to them. For instance, it is to the Greeks, and particularly Aristotle, who provided a proof of it, that we owe the discovery that the earth is spherical – though Aristotle's long tenure as the supreme authority on the physical universe obscured the achievement of **Aristarchus** (*c.* 280 BCE), who conceived of a universe in which the earth rotates not only on its own axis but also around the sun. Aristarchus was right, but Aristotle's geocentric model persisted until Copernicus, Kepler and Galileo in the fifteenth and sixteenth centuries. Aristotle's biological taxonomy was even longer-lived, as we have seen: Darwin acknowledged a profound debt to Aristotle, and philosophers today are still discussing his relevance to natural selection.

In physics and astronomy, the reductionist approach – the idea that there has to be a single source of the matter of which the world or the universe is composed – harks back to the Atomists, and even to Thales and the Milesians. Although it is contested and there is wide acceptance of its insufficiency as an explanation of complex natural processes, this approach still finds echoes in particle physicists' ongoing search for the most elementary particles of matter.

The link between contemporary atomic physics and the Presocratic Atomists looks more obvious but is more remote. Modern understanding of atomic and subatomic particles is of course very different from that of Leucippus and Democritus; but still we acknowledge their hypothesis that there existed indivisible particles of matter, which formed the building blocks of the physical world as we know it, as the distant but still recognizable ancestor of modern atomic theory.

Ethics and Society

As historians and political scientists still seek lessons for our troubled times from Athenian democracy, Greek ideas about society and governance also continue to be relevant. The continuity between the Sophists and contemporary political realist thinking is a good example. For instance, Sophistic arguments such as the notion, put forward by Thrasymachus in Plato's *Republic*, that justice is the law of the stronger are very common today: think of the slogan 'Greed is good'. Fortunately, perhaps, such definitions of good and justice are as controversial now as they were in Plato's day. So is our ongoing 'nature or nurture' debate about whether virtue and vice are innate or acquired by socialization or teaching: it appears in Plato's *Protagoras* and *Meno*. As for Aristotle, his ethics remain evergreen, still relevant to contemporary discussions of the relationship between doing good, doing right and doing well, of why we see some satisfactions in life as higher or more virtuous than others, of the purpose and limitations of social and political community.

Greek Philosophy in the Arts

The legacy of Greek thought extends far beyond the confines of philosophy and science – too far, in fact, for us to describe it in any detail. Across Renaissance Europe, art and literature were steeped in Neoplatonism and Aristotelianism: one of the most famous images of Greek philosophers is Raphael's *School of Athens*, a detail of which is on the cover of this book. Ancient Greek music theory formed the foundation of the medieval system of modes, and the musical discoveries of the Pythagoreans were regularly recounted and explored in Renaissance researches and theories on music, right up to the sixteenth-century Venetian music theoretician Gioseffo Zarlino. John Dryden invoked the Atomists in 1687 when he wrote, in *A Song for St Cecilia's Day*, of Nature, lying 'underneath a heap / Of jarring atoms' until given form and life by the harmony of the spheres. We can even see, in Plato's compelling but controversial images of a utopian society and perhaps also in the Pythagorean, Stoic and Epicurean communities, the genesis of a strong thread of imaginative literature that reaches from More's *Utopia* via Voltaire's *Candide* to Ursula Le Guin's *The Dispossessed*.

Far from being irrelevant to us, the ancient Greek philosophers still call to us vividly across 2,600 years.

Chronology

Who and When?	Where?	What Else Was Happening?
		Homer (epic poems written down c. 8th century)
		Hesiod (dates unknown, but generally agreed to have been later than Homer)
Thales (c. 625–c. 545)	Miletus, Ionia (the central region of the west coast of modern Turkey)	The Seven Sages (late 7th – early 6th century
Anaximander (c. 610–c. 540)	Miletus, Ionia	
Anaximenes (active c. 546)	Miletus, Ionia	Solon's reform of Athenian constitution (594)
Xenophanes (c. 580–c. 480)	Born Colophon, Ionia; travelled widely in Greece and Sicily	
Pythagoras (born c. 570)	Born Samos, Ionia; emigrated to Croton, thence to Metapontum (both in south of Italy)	
Heraclitus (540–475)	Ephesus, Ionia	
Parmenides (born possibly c. 515)	Elea, south Italy	Aeschylus (525/4–456), tragic dramatist
Anaxagoras (c. 500–c. 428)	Clazomenae, Ionia; moved to Athens; later fled to Lampsacus (in north-western Turkey)	Ionian Revolt (499), beginning Persian wars (first phase 498–492)
Hippasus (active first half 5th century)	Metapontum or Croton, south Italy	Persian king Xerxes invades Greece (480)
Empedocles (c. 493–c. 433)	Acragas, Sicily	Sophocles (c. 496–406), tragic dramatist
Zeno (born c. 490)	Elea, south Italy	
Protagoras (c. 485–411)	Abdera; spent most of life in Athens	Euripides (?485–?406), tragic dramatist
Gorgias (483–378)	Leontini, Sicily; well-travelled but settled in Athens	Herodotus (c. 484–c. 425)
Hippias (younger contemporary of Protagoras)	Elis	Persian Wars, second phase (480–449/8)
Antiphon (contemporary with Protagoras)	Athens	Pericles, Athenian statesman (495–429)

Who and When?	Where?	What Else Was Happening?
Socrates (c. 468–399)	Athens	
Philolaus (contemporary with Socrates)	Croton, south Italy	
Prodicus ('contemporary with Socrates')	Ceos	
Leucippus (active c. 440)	probably Miletus, Ionia	
Democritus (c. 460–370)	Abdera, Thrace	Thucydides (c. 455–c. 400)
Melissus (active 440s)	Elea, south Italy	Peloponnesian War (431–404)
Antisthenes (c. 455–c. 360)	Athens	
Thrasymachus (active c. 430–400)	Chalcedon, Bithynia (north Turkey)	Aristophanes (c. 450–c. 385)
Plato (c. 429–347)	Athens	Xenophon (c.430–c. 354)
Diogenes the Cynic (c. 400–c. 325)	Sinope, Paphlagonia (north Turkey); lived in Athens and perhaps Corinth	
Zeno of Citium (335–263)	Citium, Cyprus	
Archytas (active first half 4th century)	Tarentum, south Italy	Battle of Chaeronea, marking Macedonian conquest of Greece (338)
Aristotle (384–322)	Stagira, Chalcidice peninsula	Lamian war between Athens and Macedonia (323)
Theophrastus (372/69–288/5)	Eresus, Lesbos	Foundation of Library of Alexandria (beginning of 3rd century BCE) by Demetrius Phalereus, student of Theophrastus
Epicurus (342/1–271/70)	Samos; moved to Athens aged eighteen	
Euclid (active c. 300)	active in Alexandria	
Archimedes (c. 282–212)	Syracuse	
Chrysippus (c. 280–207)		
Lucretius (?94–?55)		
Seneca (c. 5 BCE–65 CE)		Plutarch (c. 46–c. 120 CE)
Marcus Aurelius (121–180 CE)		Diogenes Laertius (first half of 3rd century CE)
Plotinus (204/5–270 CE)	Lycopolis, Egypt	Simplicius (6th century CE)
Augustine (354–430 CE)	Hippo, Egypt	

Bold type denotes those with a specific section in the book.
All dates are necessarily approximate.

Glossary

aether The bright upper air, roughly the stratosphere, believed in Greek mythology to be the air breathed by the gods; one of the elementary substances. In Orphism, Aether was the world-soul and source of life.

axiom A proposition whose truth is taken for granted or is self-evident, and which can serve as a basis for deducing further truths.

cosmogony Account of the beginning of the universe.

cosmology Theory explaining the nature of the universe; the study of such theories.

deduction Reasoning from an axiom or general theory to more particular truths, or theorems.

dialectic The process of arriving at truth by means of question and answer, typically by exposing the flaws in another's argument. In Plato, often used to refer to the highest kind of reasoning concerned with pure ideas.

dogmatic Advancing one's own ideas as doctrine rather than submitting them to critique and questioning.

elenchus Literally, trial, cross-examination; term used to characterise Socrates' method of enquiry by eliciting an answer from an interlocutor and then testing that answer by further questions.

empirical Based on observation and experimentation rather than pure theory. An **empiricist** regards sense perception and practical experience as the only reliable sources of knowledge.

epistemology The branch of philosophy that deals with the nature, origin and scope of knowledge. From Greek *episteme*.

idealism (as a philosophical theory) The theory that the objects of sense-perception or knowledge are dependent on the activity of mind; in Plato's theory of Ideas or Forms, the theory that only ideas and mind really exist.

incommensurable (of mathematical quantities) Having no common measure; not having a common factor other than one.

induction Reasoning that uses specific observations to formulate hypotheses and thence establish general conclusions.

irrational (of numbers) Incapable of being expressed as an integer or a ratio of integers.

materialism (as a philosophical theory) The theory that only physical matter exists and that everything in the universe, including mind, thought and will, can be explained in terms of the behaviour of matter.

metaphysics The study of being, including investigation of whether we can ask whether, or what, that which is, is. What we call 'metaphysics', with reference to Greek philosophy, differs significantly from the modern discipline of metaphysics.

monism Belief in a single substance as the original and fundamental material of which the universe is composed.

music A key discipline in Greek philosophy and mathematics as well as a source of pleasure and the accompaniment to most religious and cultural pursuits, including theatre and the recitation of epic poetry. Aristoxenus (born *c.* 370 BCE) wrote the first true theory of music, the Pythagoreans being more interested in the numerical relations between intervals than in the art of music itself.

Neoplatonism A school of philosophy founded by Plotinus in the third century CE, based on the teachings of Plato and his successors. It had a strong influence on Christian and subsequently Jewish and Islamic thinkers. Suppressed in the later sixth century, it was revived in the Renaissance.

ontology The study of existence and being.

physikos One who studies the natural world (from *physis*, nature), a natural philosopher.

pluralism The belief that the universe is composed of more than one basic substance.

reductionism The philosophical view that complex systems can be understood by reducing them to their simplest components. The type of reductionism espoused by several Presocratic philosophers is called ontological reductionism —the idea that all matter consists of one or a very few basic substances in various combinations.

relativism The philosophical position that truth, knowledge and ethical values are never absolute but always relative to a culture, a point in history, or a geographical or other context.

rhetoric The art of oratory, an important discipline in Classical Greek education and a skill essential for participation in politics and law. First taught in fifth-century Athens.

scepticism A refusal to accept dogma without proof. In Greek philosophy, sceptics questioned and criticized ideas without producing or accepting doctrine, and believed that the nature of things was ultimately unknowable.

syllogism A form of deductive reasoning that derives a conclusion from two given or assumed statements (the major and minor premises).

taxonomy The classification of organisms, living and extinct; the study of systems of such classification. From *taxis*, order or arrangement.

teleology The explanation of natural phenomena with reference to their purpose; the study of design and purpose in nature; the doctrine that the material world is governed by a design or purpose. From *telos*, aim or end.

theogony Account of the origin and genealogy of the gods.

theorem A proposition that can be demonstrated by a process of deduction from an axiom.

tyranny Seizure of political power through extralegal means. In ancient Greece the word did not have the connotations of violent or repressive rule that it has today, although some tyrants certainly were violent and cruel.

universal terms, universals General concepts or terms considered axiomatic; properties, qualities or attributes (such as largeness or beauty) that are considered to be universally inherent in the particular members of classes of things.

zoogony Account of the origin of living creatures/animals.

Further Reading

There is a vast body of works on the Ancient Greek philosophers and their world. I mention here a few of the available edited translations and commentaries, including some which I have consulted in the preparation of this book. They represent only the very tip of the iceberg.

Annas, Julia. *Plato: A Very Short Introduction.* (Oxford: Oxford University Press, 2003). Introduces the main topics of Plato's thought concisely and readably.

Barnes, Jonathan (ed.). *Complete Works of Aristotle: The Revised Oxford Translation* (Princeton: Princeton University Press, 1984)

Barnes, Jonathan. *Aristotle: A Very Short Introduction* (Oxford: Oxford University Press, 2000). As with the Plato VSI, a brief and readable introduction, but rather more technical in approach.

Barnes, Jonathan. *Early Greek Philosophy*, 2nd edn (London: Penguin, 2001). Brings together all the significant fragments of the Presocratics, with useful introductory notes and guidance to the provenance of the fragments.

Cooper, John M. (ed.). *Complete Works, Plato, Edited with Introduction and Notes* (Indianapolis: Hackett, 1997)

Fearn, Nicholas. *Zeno and the Tortoise: How to Think Like a Philosopher* (London: Atlantic Books, 2001). A book about thinking rather than a history, but with some good expositions of key moments in Ancient Greek thought.

Guthrie, W. K. C. *A History of Greek Philosophy* (6 vols, Cambridge: Cambridge University Press, 1962–81). The classic general history of Greek philosophy.

Russell, Bertrand. *History of Western Philosophy*, 2nd edn (Unwin Paperbacks, 1981). A classic of philosophy; more recent scholarship has overtaken it, but still a wonderfully readable introduction.

Sharples, R. W. *Stoics, Epicureans and Sceptics: An Introduction to Hellenistic Philosophy* (London: Routledge, 1996). Organized by theme, accessible to readers new to the field as well as those with some previous knowledge.

Also, affordable recent translations of many major figures in Greek philosophy are published by Penguin.

Index

Abdera, Thrace 87, 96, 162, 163
Acragas 40, 79
Aeschylus 162
aether 164
akousmata (aphorisms) 55, 65
Alexander the Great 32, 131
Alexandria 19, 154, 163
Amphipolis 37
Anaxagoras 50, 79, 84–7, 88, 90, 95, 138, 162
Anaximander 40, 41, 42, 46–9, 51, 57, 62, 162
Anaximenes 40, 41, 45, 49–50, 51, 162
Andronicus 156
Antiphon 100, 162
Antisthenes 148, 149, 163
apeiron ('the boundless') 46–7, 51, 86
Aphorists 58
Archimedes 156, 163
Archytas of Tarentum 58, 163
Aristarchus 159
Aristophanes 17, 103, 163
Aristotelianism 160
Aristotle 12, 14, 18, 19–20, 31, 32, 36, 38, 40, 41, 44, 46, 54, 64, 67, 72, 74, 75, 76, 88, 89, 90, 99, 130–47, 150, 154, 156–60, 163
Aristotle's Lyceum 154
Aristoxenus 164
arts, Greek philosophy in the 160–61
Asia Minor 24, 26, 37, 59, 131
astronomy 159
Athens 19, 26, 28, 32, 37, 40, 67, 84, 93, 96, 98, 115, 116, 162, 163, 164
atomic theory 159
atomism 87, 91, 127
Atomists 40, 73, 79, 87–90, 140, 159
Attica 28
Augustine 155, 163
axiom 136, 164

Babylonia 18, 36, 45
Babylonians 9, 18
Barnes, Jonathan 138

beauty 29, 110, 122
Bias of Priene 36
biological researches (Aristotle) 140–41
Burkert, Walter 53

Calippus 145
Callisthenes 131
causation 133, 137, 139–40, 145, 147
cave analogy 114–15, 129
Ceos 163
Chalcis, Euboaea 132
change 63–4, 68, 77
Charmides 104, 115
Chilon of Sparta 27–8, 36
Chinese 19
Christians, Christianity 64, 155
Chrysippus 150, 163
city-states 25–8, 30, 32, 110, 144
classification 132, 133, 141, 147
Clazomenae, Ionia 40, 84, 162
Cleobulus of Lindus 36
Colophon, Ionia 40, 162
condensation 45, 49–50, 51
conservation, laws of 65
Copernicus, Nicolaus 159
Corinth 96
cosmic justice 42, 47–8, 62, 63
cosmogony 83, 164
Crates 149
Critchley, Simon 107–8
Critias 104, 115
Croesus, King 44
Croton, southern Italy 40, 54, 162, 163
Cynicism 8, 153
Cynics 32, 148–9, 151

Darwin, Charles 159
deduction 164
Delphic oracle 108
Demetrius Phalereus 163
democracy 11, 36, 93, 104, 106, 125, 160
Democritus of Abdera 40, 50, 79, 84, 87–90, 96, 138, 159, 163
Descartes, René 134

dialectic 108, 113, 129, 164
Diogenes Laertius 19, 31, 44, 54, 67, 152, 163
Diogenes the Cynic 148, 149
Dion 115–16
Dionysus cult 34
Dorians 24, 26

Egypt 18, 36, 37, 42
Egyptians, ancient 9, 18
Elea, southern Italy 40, 66, 67, 162, 163
Eleatics 40, 63, 67–77, 95
elenchus (cross-examination) 108–9, 127, 164
Empedocles 33, 73, 79–83, 99
empirical 164
empiricism, empiricist 78, 135, 164
Ephesus, Ionia (modern Efes, Turkey) 40, 61, 162
Epicureans, Epicureanism 150, 152–3, 155, 161
Epicurus 90, 152–3, 163
epistemology 1764
ethics 8, 12, 14–15, 94, 142–3, 147
  and society 160
Euclid 156, 163
eudaimonia (happiness) 121, 142, 143, 144
Eudoxus 145
Euripides 17, 34, 162
evolution 48, 82

fire 63, 64, 65
first philosophy 134, 144–6
Forms, theory of 15, 69, 114, 120, 125–9, 130, 147, 149, 150
four elements 47–8, 80–83, 91, 127, 145
Frege, Gottlob 158

Galileo Galilei 134, 159
geometry 58
good and evil 8, 10, 35, 110
goodness 94, 95, 105, 120, 142, 146
Gorgias 92, 94, 98–9, 148, 162

Halicarnassus, Ionia 36
harmonic mean 58
harmonics 58
Hellenistic philosophy and science 154–7
Heraclitus 11–12, 15, 17, 20, 42, 61–5, 66, 67, 68, 84, 88, 90, 150, 162
Herodotus 17, 31, 36–7, 44, 162
Hesiod 16, 22, 25, 26, 33, 162
Hesiodic poems 60
Hippasus of Croton 58, 162
Hippias 100, 162
Homer 23, 33, 55, 59, 162
Homeric epics 22, 23–5, 60

idealism 95, 116, 164
incommensurable 164
induction 137, 164
injustice 110
Ionia, Ionians 18, 40, 52
'irrational' numbers 42, 164
Italy 25, 40, 52

justice 15, 35, 94–7, 100, 105, 106, 110, 111, 113, 117, 129, 151, 160
Justinian, Emperor 116

Kepler, Johannes 159
knowledge 10, 65, 69, 94, 98, 101, 105, 108, 110, 112, 113, 117, 121, 129, 134–5, 136, 144, 147, 150
kosmos 42

Lampsacus, Turkey 40, 84, 153, 162
legacy of Greek philosophy 157–8
Leucippus 79, 84, 87–90, 159, 163
logic 12, 14, 68, 69, 71, 73, 135–6, 147, 158
logical paradoxes 73–6, 77, 90
logos 64, 65, 69, 150–51
love 105, 110, 117, 121, 146, 81, 82, 91
Lucretius 90, 153, 163
Lycurgus 27
Lydia 43, 45

Macedonia 131, 163

Macedonians 28, 154
Marcus Aurelius 152, 163
materialism 164
Mathematicians 58
mean, the 143
Megara 115
Melissus 72–3, 77, 163
Ménage, Gilles 31
metaphysics 12, 15, 144, 164
Metapontum, south of Italy 54, 162
meteorology 61
Middle East 18
Milesians 40, 43–51, 52, 55, 60, 63, 84, 156, 159
Miletus, Ionia 24, 40, 43, 45, 162, 163
mind and matter 10
moderation 133–4
monism, monists 51, 73, 76, 77, 78, 158, 164
Montaigne, Michel de 61
morality, moral values 14, 94, 96, 100, 101, 111, 112, 113, 117, 120
More, Sir Thomas 161
music 42, 53, 54, 57, 65, 161, 164
'music of the spheres' 56
Mycenaeans 24
Myson of Chenae 36
Mytilene, Lesbos 153

'natural philosophers' 11, 12
natural sciences 158–9
natural selection 139, 159
nature
  harmony with 151, 153
  laws of 10
Neoplatonism 154, 155, 160, 164
Nichomachus 142
Nietzsche, Friedrich 68, 70
Nous 86, 87, 91

oneness theory 15, 66, 67, 68, 71, 74, 77
ontological reductionism 164
ontology 15, 164
opposites 47, 62–3, 64, 65
Orphism 33–4, 71, 164

Parmenides 14, 15, 40, 63, 66, 67–73, 74, 76, 77, 78, 80, 84, 88, 90, 162

Pericles 37, 84, 93, 96, 162
Persia, Persians 43, 93
Philip of Macedon 32, 131
Philolaus 58, 163
philosopher–kings 123, 124–5, 129, 143
Phoenicia 17
physics 12–13, 159
physikos 164
Pittacus of Mytilene 36
Plato 10, 15, 17, 18–19, 28, 30–31, 32, 34, 36, 39, 40, 41, 54, 58, 64, 65, 67, 69, 72, 73, 74, 90, 92, 94–100, 102–6, 109–12, 114–29, 130, 131, 132, 135, 143, 149, 150, 157, 160, 161, 164
Platonic dialogues 118–19
Platonic relationship 122
Platonism 117, 128
Plato's Academy, Athens 116, 128, 130, 131, 153, 154
Pliny 45
Plotinus 154, 163, 164
pluralism, pluralists 40, 78, 85, 158, 164
Plutarch 27, 31, 163
political theory 8
politics 35, 143–4, 147
Presocratic philosophers 14–17, 19, 32–3, 35, 37, 38–51, 53, 78, 79, 120, 144, 164
Prodicus 100, 162
Protagoras 92, 94, 96–8, 162
Pythagoras 31, 42, 43, 52–5, 58, 59, 65, 79, 157, 162
Pythagoras' theorem 52, 53, 57–8, 65
Pythagoreanism 52
Pythagoreans 15, 31, 34, 40–43, 52–8, 62, 65, 83, 156, 161, 164

rarefaction 45, 50, 51
reality 117, 129
reductionism 159, 164
relativism 95, 97, 99, 101, 112, 164
religion 59–60, 64, 65, 97, 107–8
rhetoric 164
Russell, Bertrand 8, 10, 24, 42, 69, 100–101

Salamis 93
Samos, Ionia 40, 54, 72, 162, 163
sceptics, scepticism 98, 100, 111, 165
science 8, 11, 16, 19, 134, 138
seeds of matter 85, 86, 88, 91
Seneca 152, 163
sense-perception 147, 150
Seven Sages, The 27, 36, 44, 115, 162
Sicily 25, 40, 59, 98, 115, 162
Simplicius 19, 67, 72, 88, 163
sociology 12
Socrates 15, 17, 18, 19, 36, 38–9, 67, 74, 94, 102–13, 115, 116, 117, 119–20, 121, 124, 125, 148, 163, 164
Socratic method 108–9, 128
Solon of Athens 28, 36, 115, 162
Sophism, Sophists 15, 29, 39, 40, 92–101, 108, 160
soul, the 17, 35, 43, 46, 54, 55, 106, 109, 112, 113, 117, 121, 123, 129
transmigration of souls 53, 83, 109
Sparta 24, 26–8, 32, 37, 96, 104, 125
Speusippus 116

Stagira 130, 163
Stoa, Athens 149, 153
Stoicism 8, 149, 153, 155
Stoics 32, 64, 149–52, 155, 156, 161
Strife 62, 63, 81–2, 91
Sullivan, Shirley Darcus 71
Sybaris, southern Italy 44
syllogism 136–7, 165
Syracuse 116, 125, 163

taxonomy 141, 159, 165
teleology 133, 138, 139, 165
telos 138, 139, 141, 142, 147
Thales 14, 16, 18, 30, 36, 38, 40, 41, 44–6, 47, 49, 50, 51, 159, 162
Thebes 149
theogony 165
'theology' 134, 144
Theophrastus 163
theorem 165
theos (the divine) 64
Thirty Tyrants 104, 115
Thrace 33, 37, 43
Thrasymachus 100, 163
Thucydides 17, 36, 37, 163
truth 98, 100–101, 108, 113, 137, 150
tyranny 165

universal principles 110–11, 113

universal terms, universals 145, 165
universe
    a closed sphere 80, 91
    harmony of the 57
    nature of the 8, 10, 12, 13, 15, 16, 30, 35, 38, 41–2, 78
    one material as its basis 14, 45, 159
'unmoved mover' 146, 147

vegetarianism 83
virtue(s) 94–5, 97, 110–13, 120, 121, 124, 129, 142, 143, 151, 153
Voltaire 161

Williams, Bernard 157
wisdom 106, 108, 113, 121
women philosophers 31

Xenophanes of Colophon 52, 54, 59–61, 64, 65, 67, 84, 88, 162
Xenophon 102–3, 105, 163
Xerxes 84, 162

Zeno of Citium 149, 150, 163
Zeno of Elea 40, 66, 73–5, 77, 78, 85, 90, 99, 162
zoogony 83, 165

Acknowledgements

Several people have helped me in this project with valuable comments and thought-provoking discussions; but I am most deeply indebted to Dr Peter Caldwell of the University of Technology, Sydney, who patiently read through drafts and whose wise insights have made this a much better book.

To avoid cluttering the text with notes, I have listed under 'Further Reading' several of the modern works on Greek philosophy from which I have quoted. In particular, for quotations from the Presocratic philosophers I have relied with very few exceptions on Jonathan Barnes's translations in his *Early Greek Philosophy* (2nd edn, London, Penguin, 2001).

The quotation from Nietzsche on p.66 is from his *Philosophy in the Tragic Age of the Greeks*, translated, with an introduction, by Marianne Cowan (Washington, DC: Regnery Gateway, 1962).

The quotation from Shirley Darcus Sullivan on p.71 is from her *Psychological and Ethical Ideas: What Ancient Greeks Say* (Leiden & New York: E.J. Brill, 1995).

The quotation from Hegel on p.102 is from his *Lectures on the History of Philosophy*, translated by E.S. Haldane (Lincoln, Nebraska: University of Nebraska Press, 1995).

The quotation from Bernard Williams on p.157 is from his *Shame and Necessity* (Berkeley: University of California Press, 1994).